This Book Belong To:

Date: _____ ◷ Time: _____
 Location: _____

Weather Conditions

☀ ☁ ⛅ 🌧 🌧 🌨 🚩 🌡
☐ ☐ ☐ ☐ ☐ ☐ ☐ _____ _____

Firearm:	
Bullet:	Seating Depth:
Powder:	Grains:
Primer:	
Brass:	
Distance:	

Overall Results

☐ Poor   ☐ Fair   ☐ Good   ☐ Excellent

Notes

_____
_____
_____

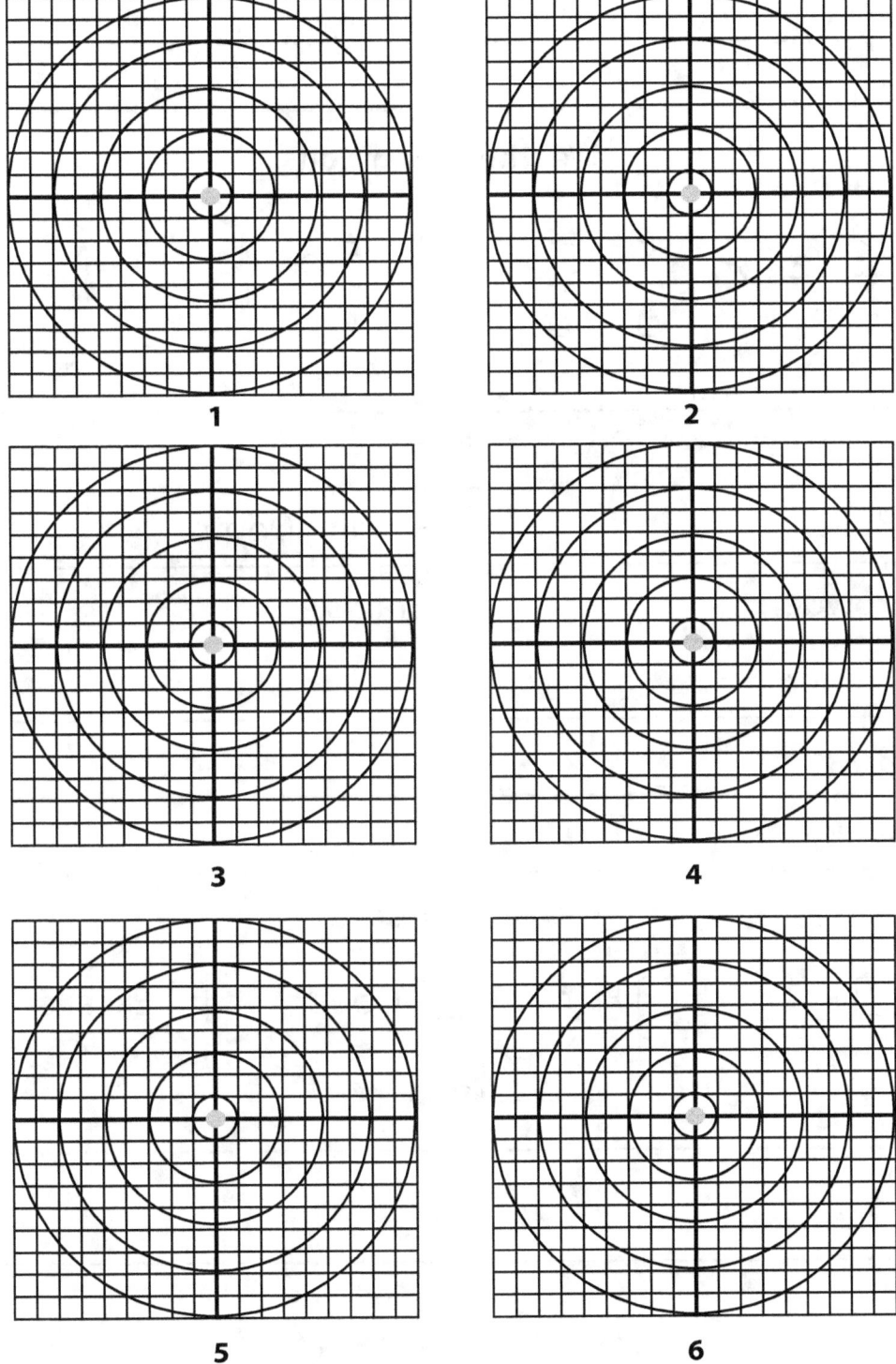

📅 Date: _____ 🕐 Time: _____

📍 Location: _____

Weather Conditions

☀️ ☐   ☁️ ☐   ⛅ ☐   🌧️ ☐   🌧️ ☐   🌨️ ☐   🚩 _____   🌡️ _____

Firearm:	
Bullet:	Seating Depth:
Powder:	Grains:
Primer:	
Brass:	
Distance:	

Overall Results

☐ Poor   ☐ Fair   ☐ Good   ☐ Excellent

Notes

_____

_____

_____

☆ ☆ ☆ ☆ ☆

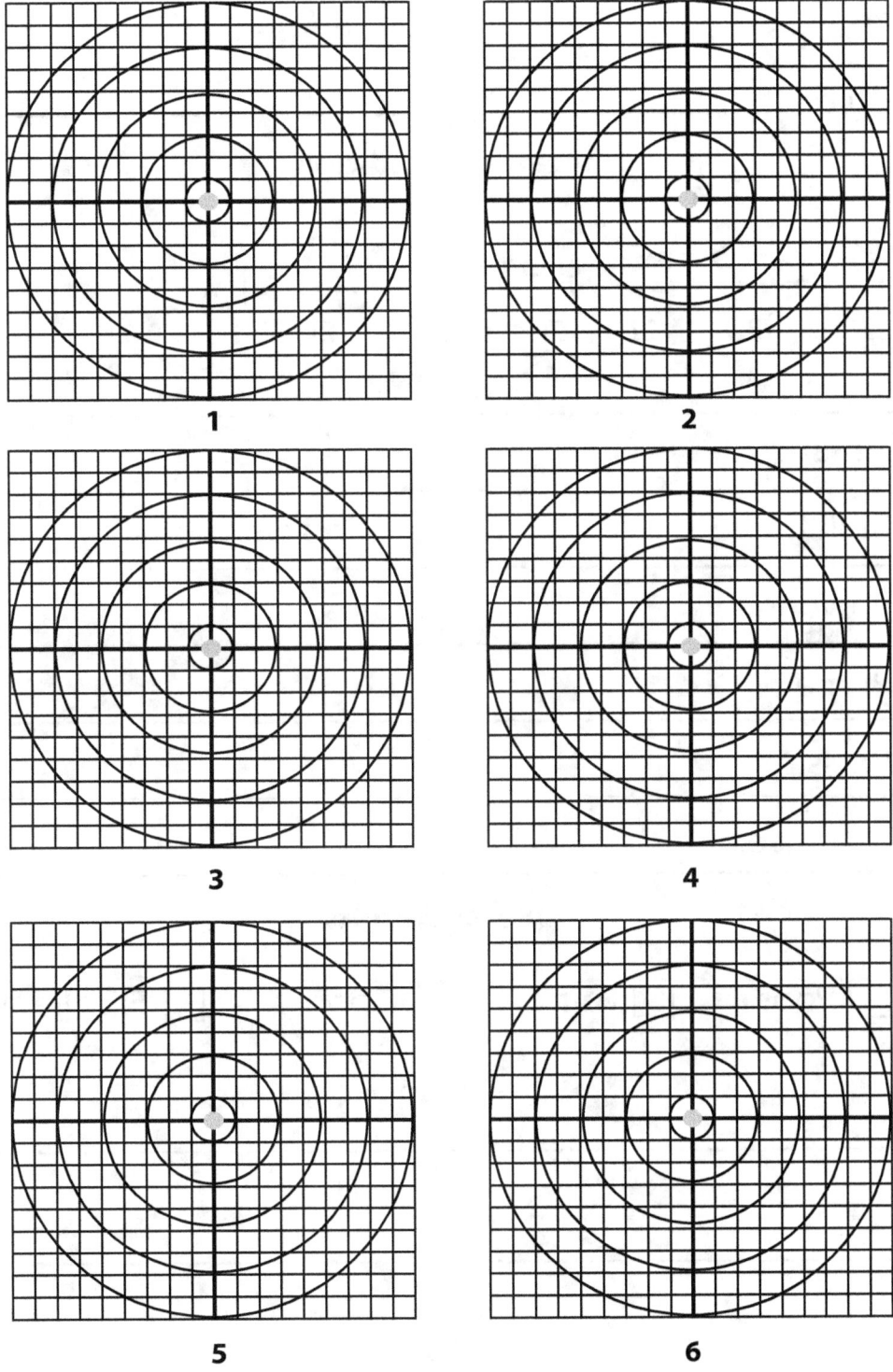

📅 Date: _____ 🕐 Time: _____

📍 Location: _____

Weather Conditions

☀️ ☁️ ⛅ 🌦️ 🌧️ 🌨️ 🚩 _____ 🌡️ _____
☐   ☐   ☐   ☐   ☐   ☐

Firearm:	
Bullet:	Seating Depth:
Powder:	Grains:
Primer:	
Brass:	
Distance:	

Overall Results

☐ Poor   ☐ Fair   ☐ Good   ☐ Excellent

Notes

_____

_____

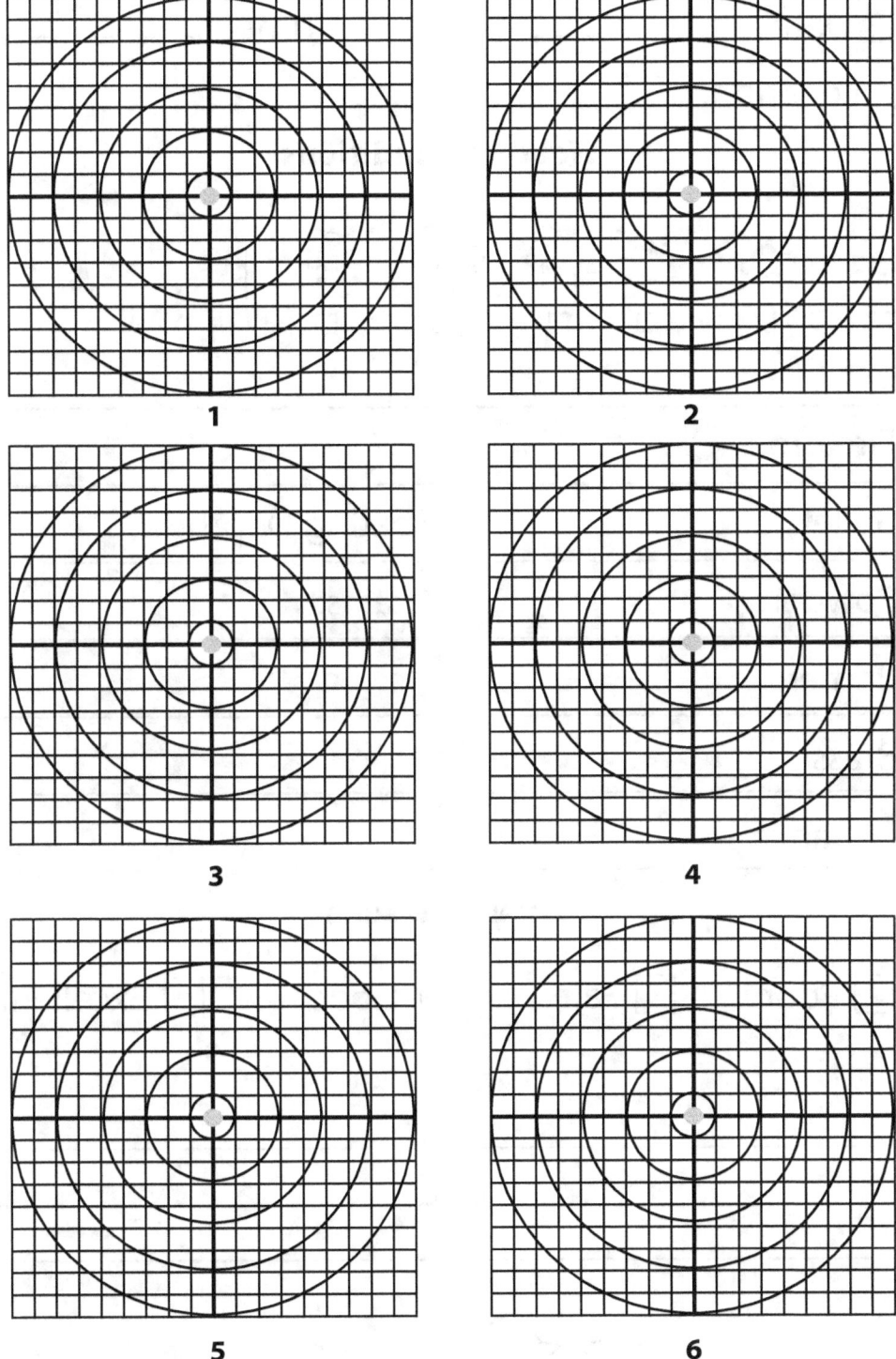

Date: _____   Time: _____

 Location: _____

Weather Conditions

☀ ☁ ⛅ 🌧 🌧 🌨 🚩 🌡
☐ ☐ ☐ ☐ ☐ ☐ ___ ___

Firearm:	
Bullet:	Seating Depth:
Powder:	Grains:
Primer:	
Brass:	
Distance:	

Overall Results

☐ Poor   ☐ Fair   ☐ Good   ☐ Excellent

Notes

_____
_____
_____

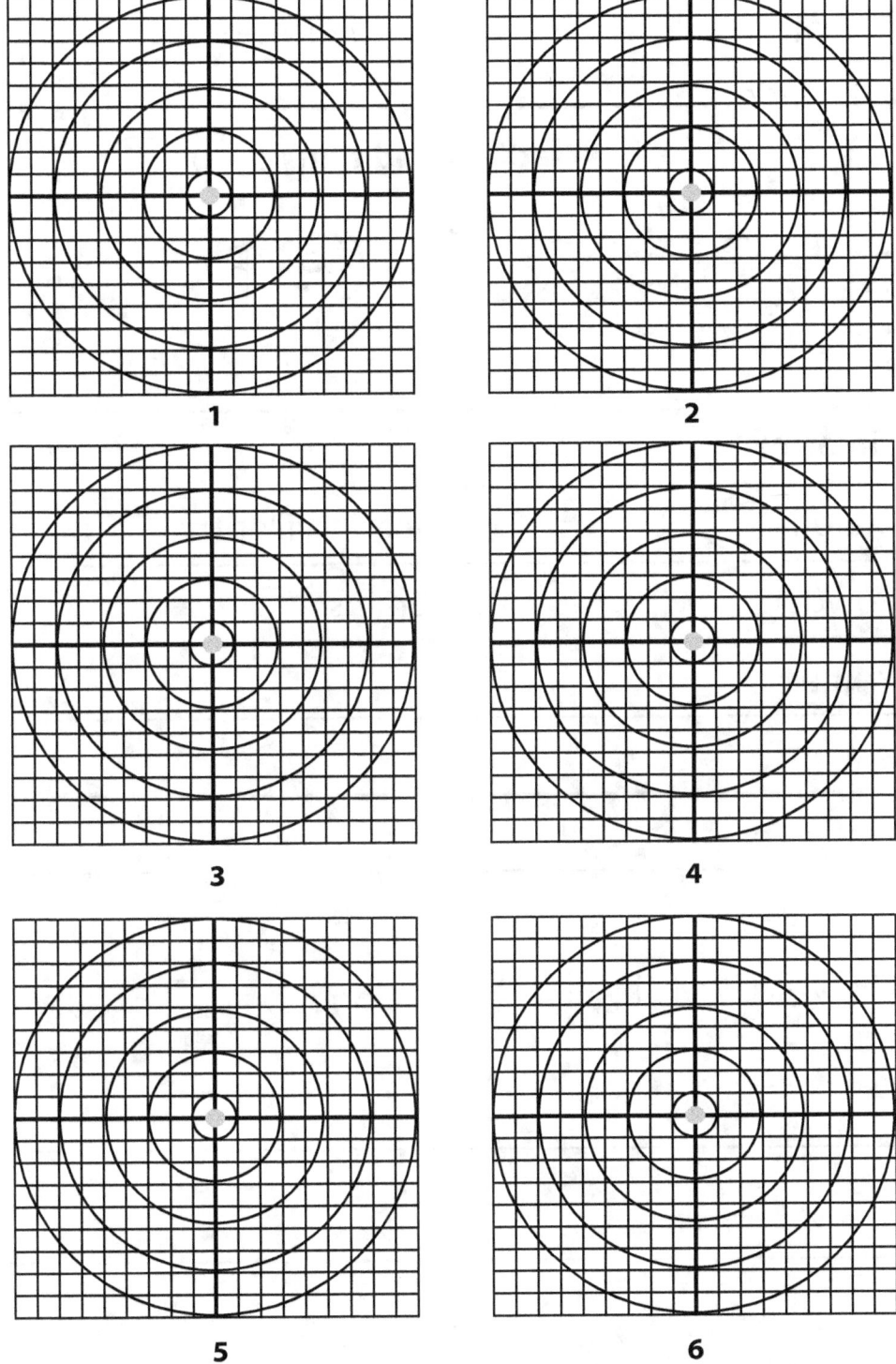

📅 Date: _____ 🕐 Time: _____

📍 Location: _____

Weather Conditions

☀ ☁ ⛅ 🌦 🌧 🌨 🚩 🌡
☐ ☐ ☐ ☐ ☐ ☐ _____ _____

Firearm:	
Bullet:	Seating Depth:
Powder:	Grains:
Primer:	
Brass:	
Distance:	

Overall Results

☐ Poor   ☐ Fair   ☐ Good   ☐ Excellent

Notes

_____
_____
_____

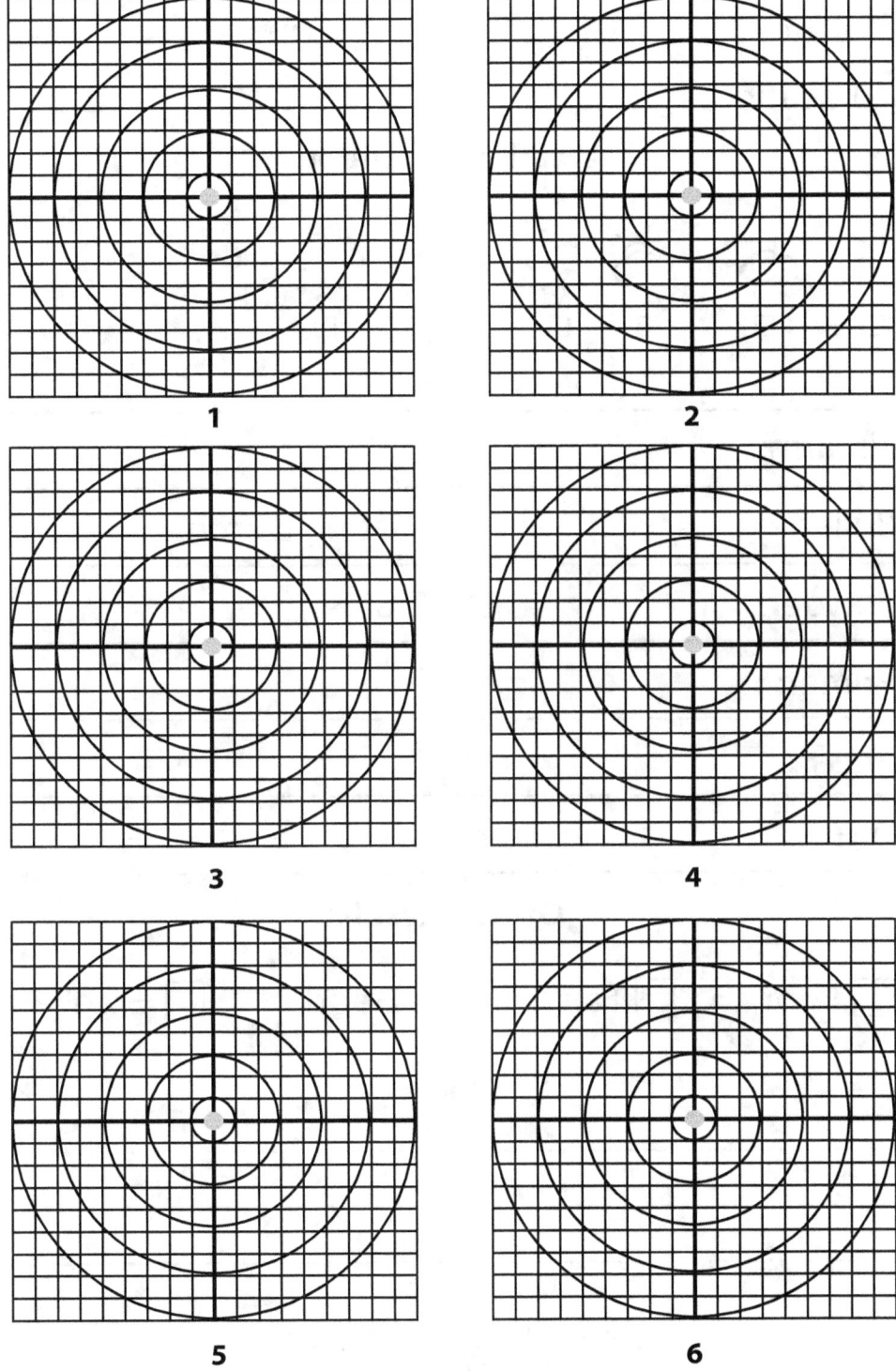

Date: _____ Time: _____
Location: _____

Weather Conditions

☀ ☁ 🌥 🌦 🌧 🌨 🚩 _____ 🌡 _____
☐ ☐ ☐ ☐ ☐ ☐

Firearm:	
Bullet:	Seating Depth:
Powder:	Grains:
Primer:	
Brass:	
Distance:	

Overall Results

☐ Poor ☐ Fair ☐ Good ☐ Excellent

Notes

_____
_____
_____

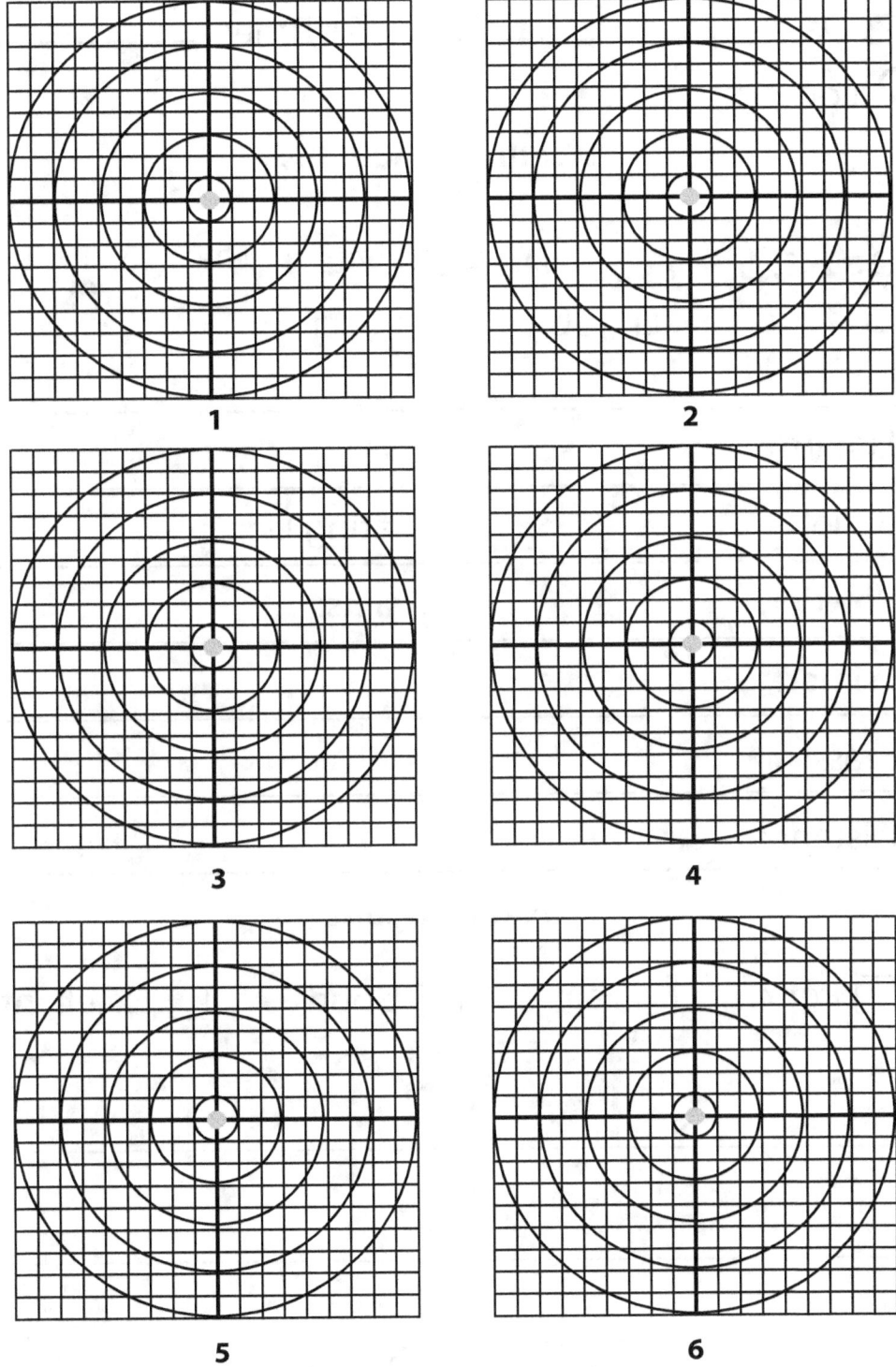

📅 Date: _____ 🕐 Time: _____

📍 Location: _____

Weather Conditions

☀ ☁ 🌤 🌥 🌧 🌨 🚩
☐ ☐ ☐ ☐ ☐ ☐ _____ _____

Firearm:	
Bullet:	Seating Depth:
Powder:	Grains:
Primer:	
Brass:	
Distance:	

Overall Results

☐ Poor   ☐ Fair   ☐ Good   ☐ Excellent

Notes

_____
_____
_____

☆ ☆ ☆ ☆ ☆

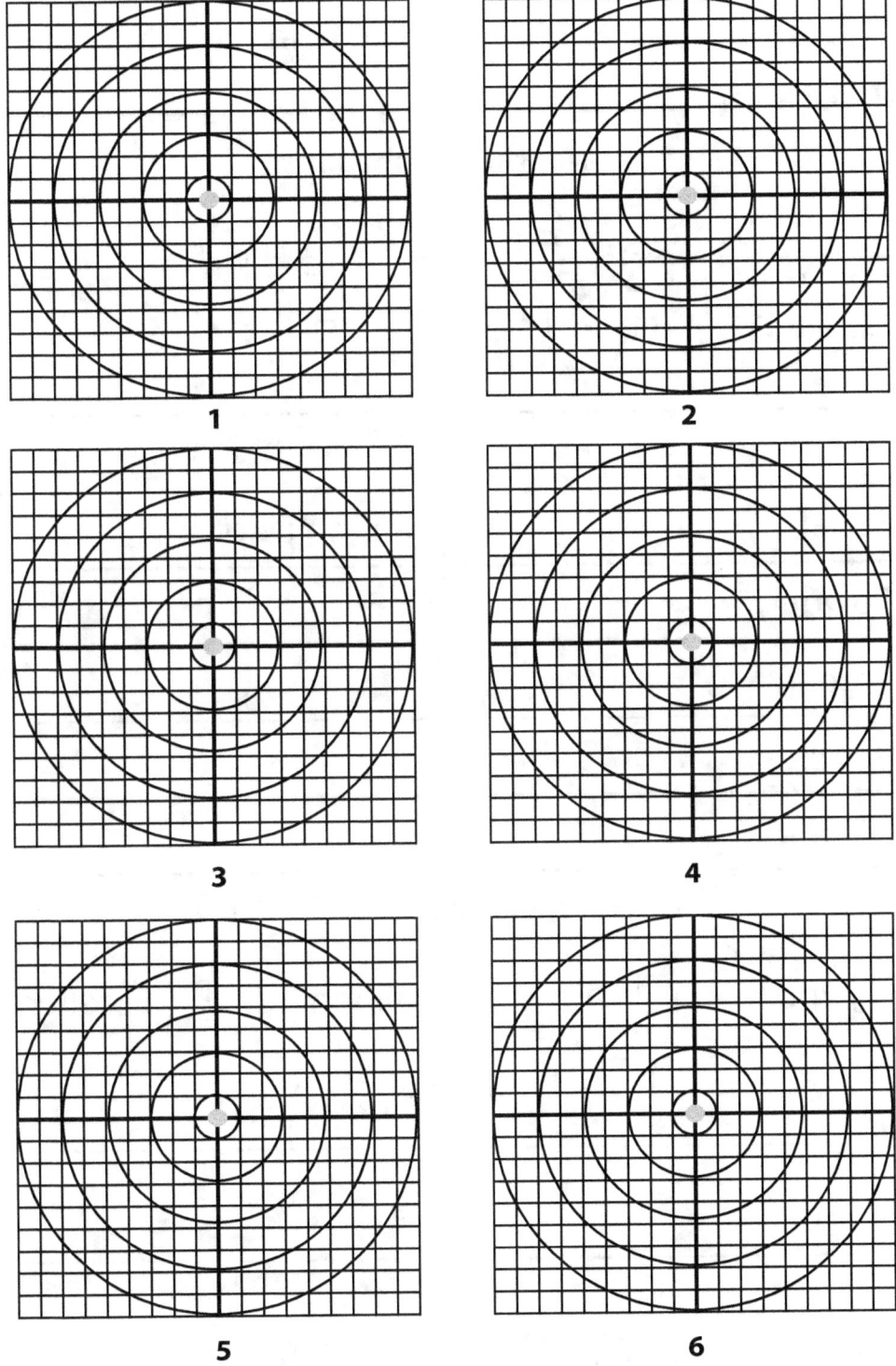

Date: _____   Time: _____
Location: _____

Weather Conditions

☀ ☁ ⛅ 🌧 🌧 🌨 🚩 🌡
☐ ☐ ☐ ☐ ☐ ☐

Firearm:	
Bullet:	Seating Depth:
Powder:	Grains:
Primer:	
Brass:	
Distance:	

Overall Results

☐ Poor   ☐ Fair   ☐ Good   ☐ Excellent

Notes

_____
_____
_____

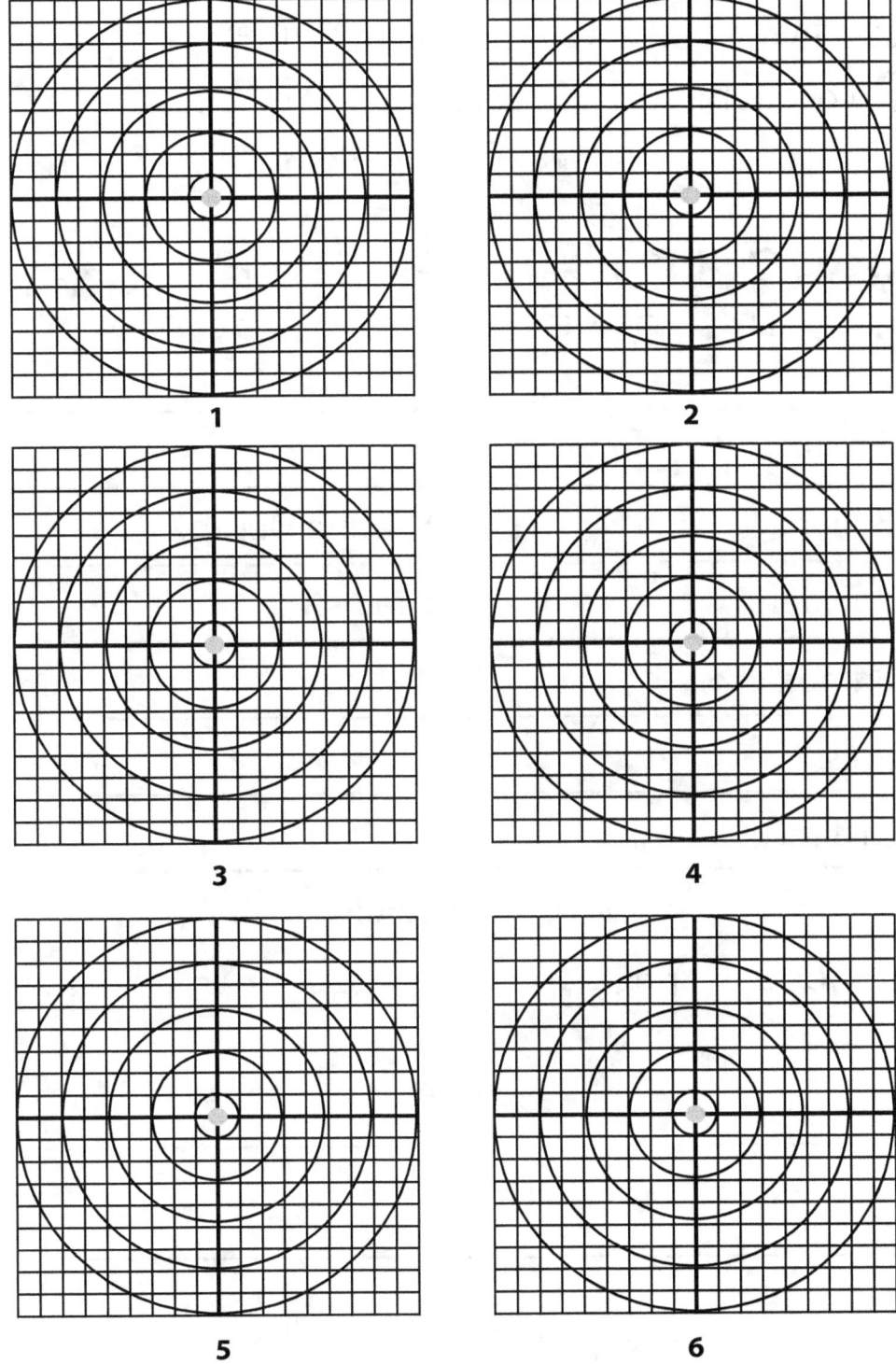

📅 Date: _____ 🕐 Time: _____

📍 Location: _____

Weather Conditions

☀️ ☁️ ⛅ 🌧️ 🌧️ 🌨️ 🚩 🌡️
☐ ☐ ☐ ☐ ☐ ☐ ___ ___

Firearm:	
Bullet:	Seating Depth:
Powder:	Grains:
Primer:	
Brass:	
Distance:	

Overall Results

☐ Poor   ☐ Fair   ☐ Good   ☐ Excellent

Notes

_____
_____
_____

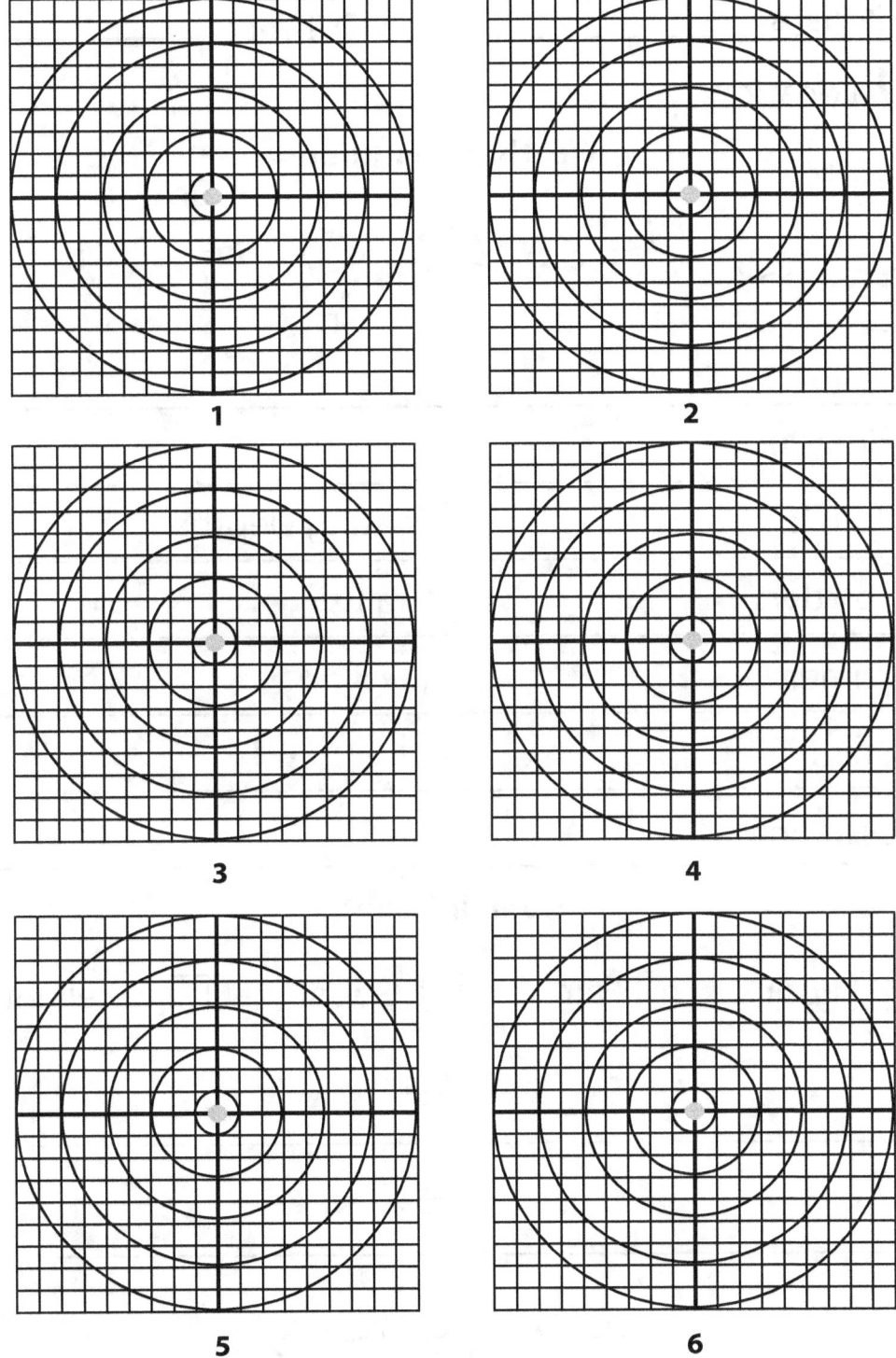

Date: _____ ⏱ Time: _____
 ♀ Location: _____

Weather Conditions

☀ ☁ ☁ ☁ ☁ ☁ ⚑ 🌡
☐ ☐ ☐ ☐ ☐ ☐ _____

Firearm:	
Bullet:	Seating Depth:
Powder:	Grains:
Primer:	
Brass:	
Distance:	

Overall Results

☐ Poor   ☐ Fair   ☐ Good   ☐ Excellent

Notes

_____
_____
_____

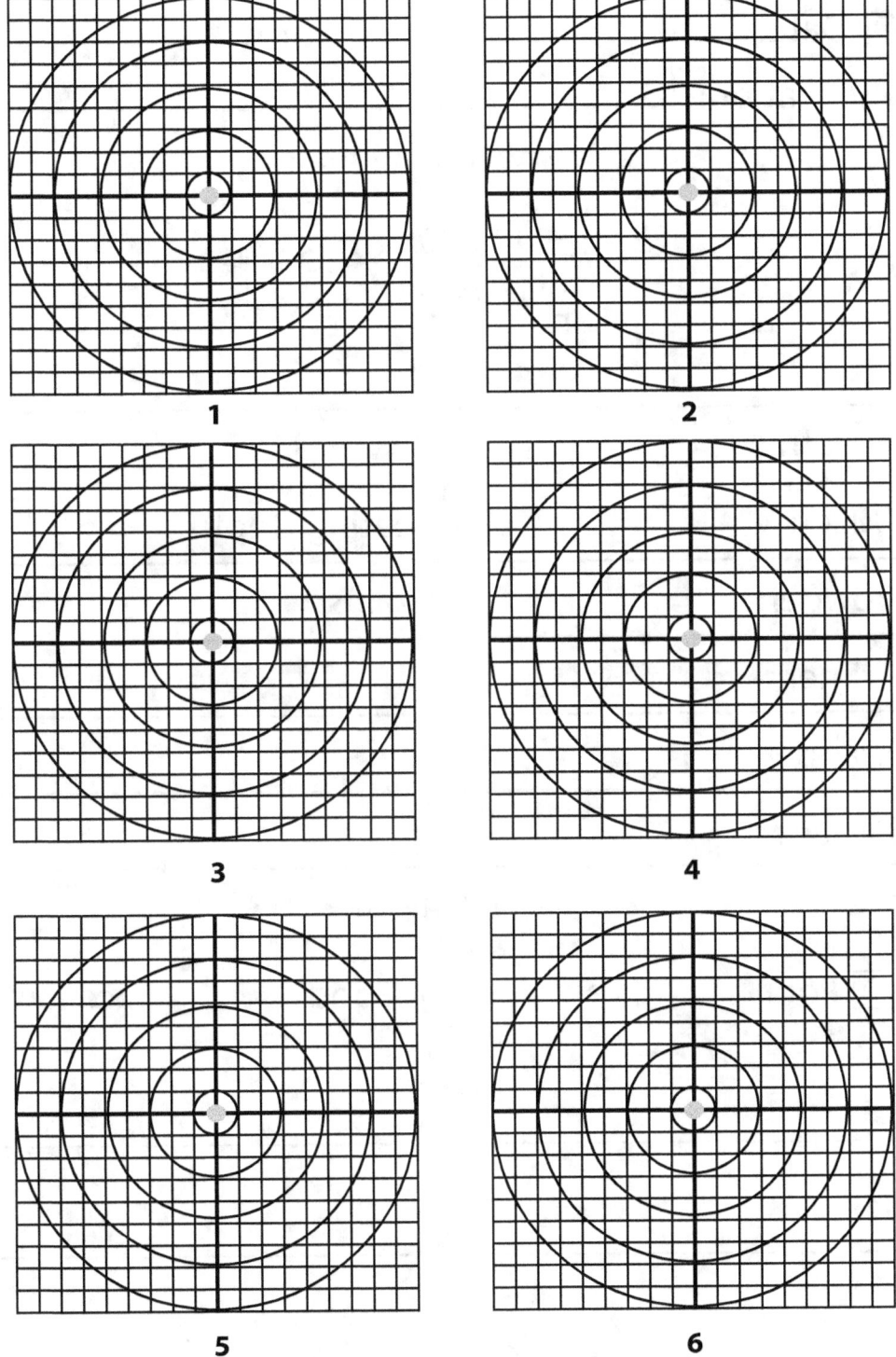

Date: _____   Time: _____

  Location: _____

Weather Conditions

☀ ☁ ⛅ 🌧 🌧 ❄ 🚩 🌡
☐ ☐ ☐ ☐ ☐ ☐

Firearm:	
Bullet:	Seating Depth:
Powder:	Grains:
Primer:	
Brass:	
Distance:	

Overall Results

☐ Poor   ☐ Fair   ☐ Good   ☐ Excellent

Notes

_____

_____

_____

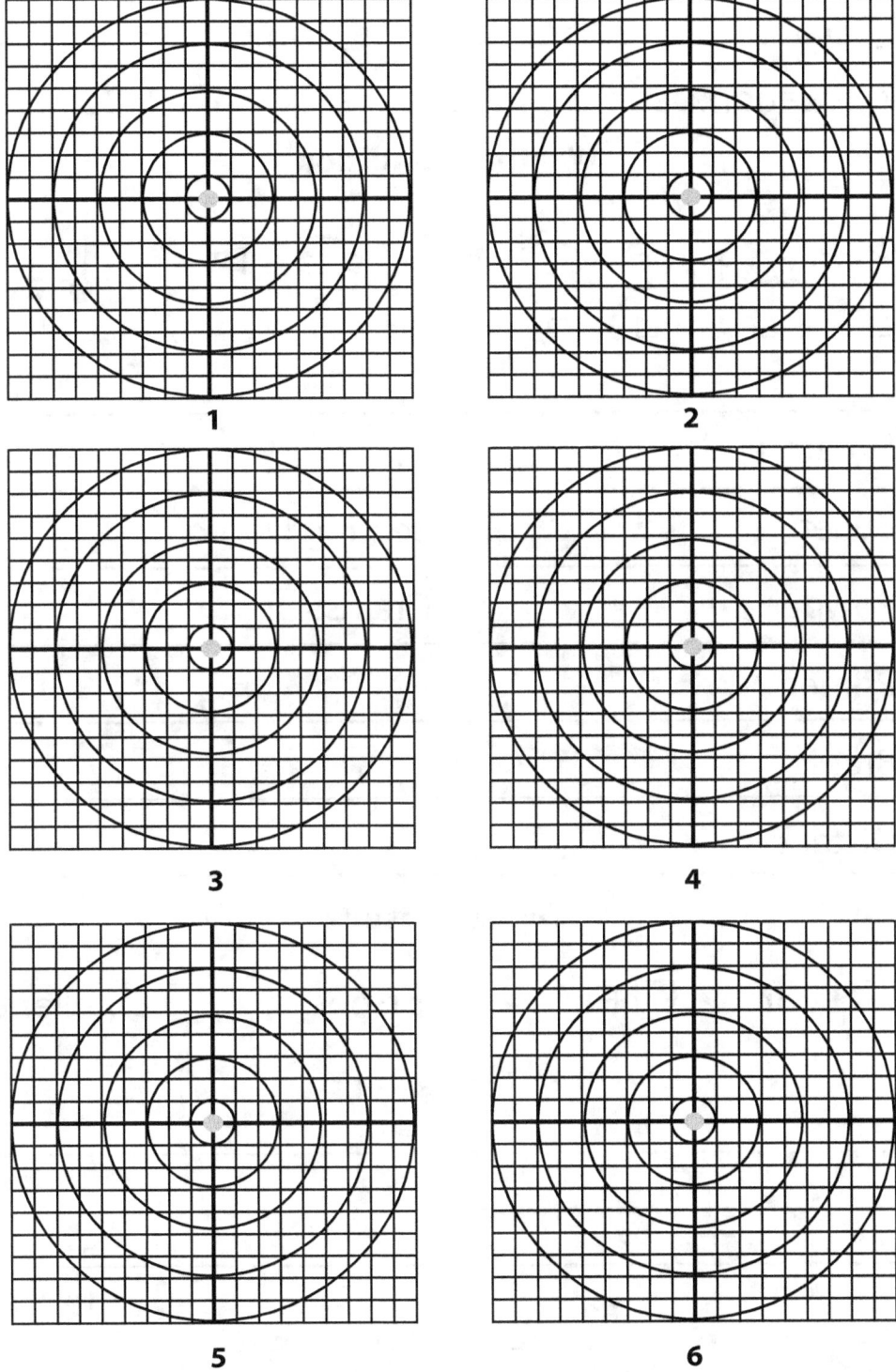

Date: _____ **Time:** _____

Location: _____

Weather Conditions

☀️ ☁️ ⛅ 🌧️ 🌧️ 🌨️ 🚩 🌡️
☐   ☐   ☐   ☐   ☐   ☐   _____ _____

Firearm:	
Bullet:	Seating Depth:
Powder:	Grains:
Primer:	
Brass:	
Distance:	

Overall Results

☐ Poor   ☐ Fair   ☐ Good   ☐ Excellent

Notes

_____
_____
_____

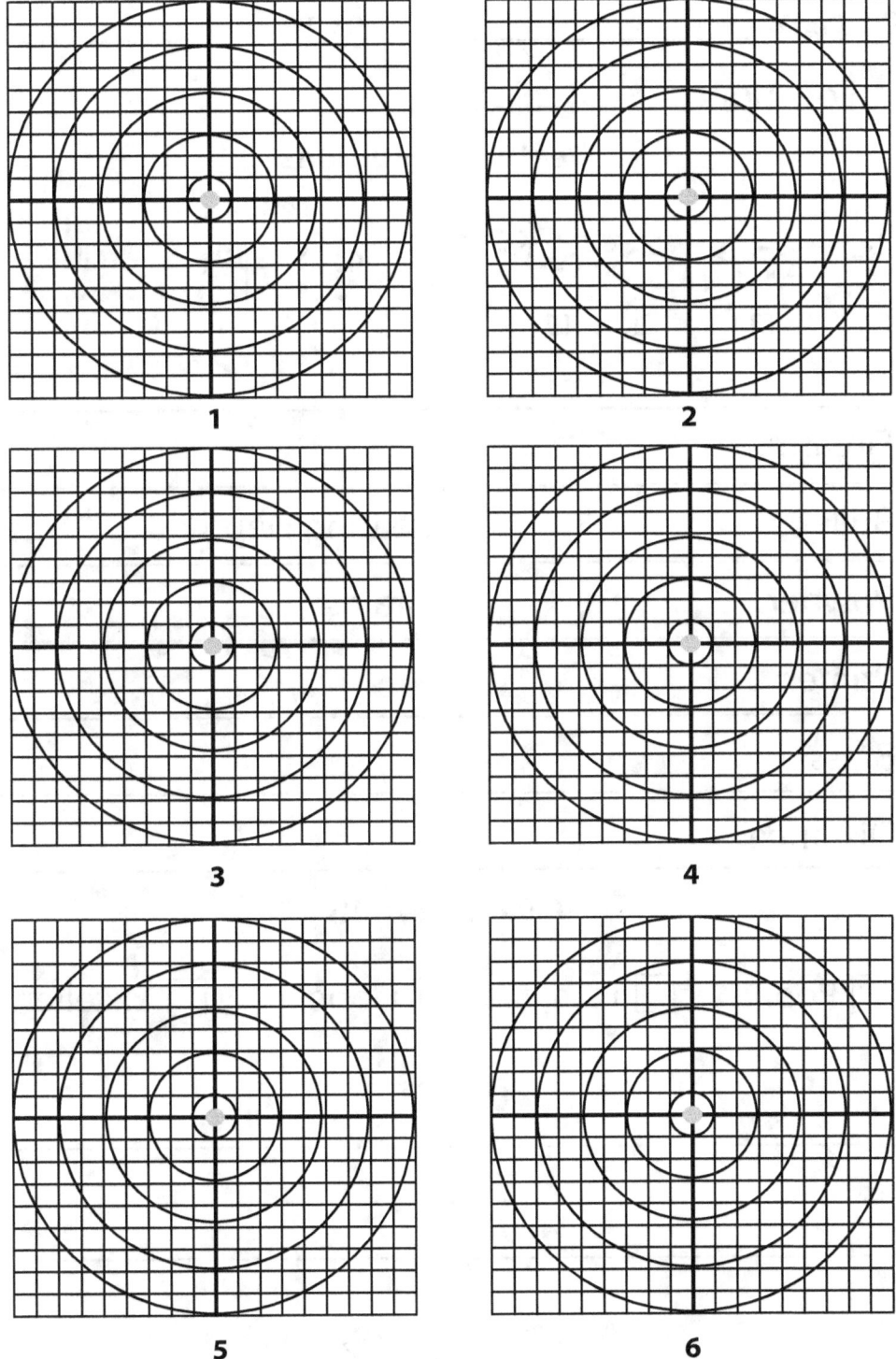

Date: _____   Time: _____
 Location: _____

Weather Conditions

☀ ☁ ☁ ☁ ☁ ☁ 🚩 🌡
☐ ☐ ☐ ☐ ☐ ☐ _____ _____

Firearm:	
Bullet:	Seating Depth:
Powder:	Grains:
Primer:	
Brass:	
Distance:	

Overall Results

☐ Poor   ☐ Fair   ☐ Good   ☐ Excellent

Notes

_____
_____
_____

☆ ☆ ☆ ☆ ☆

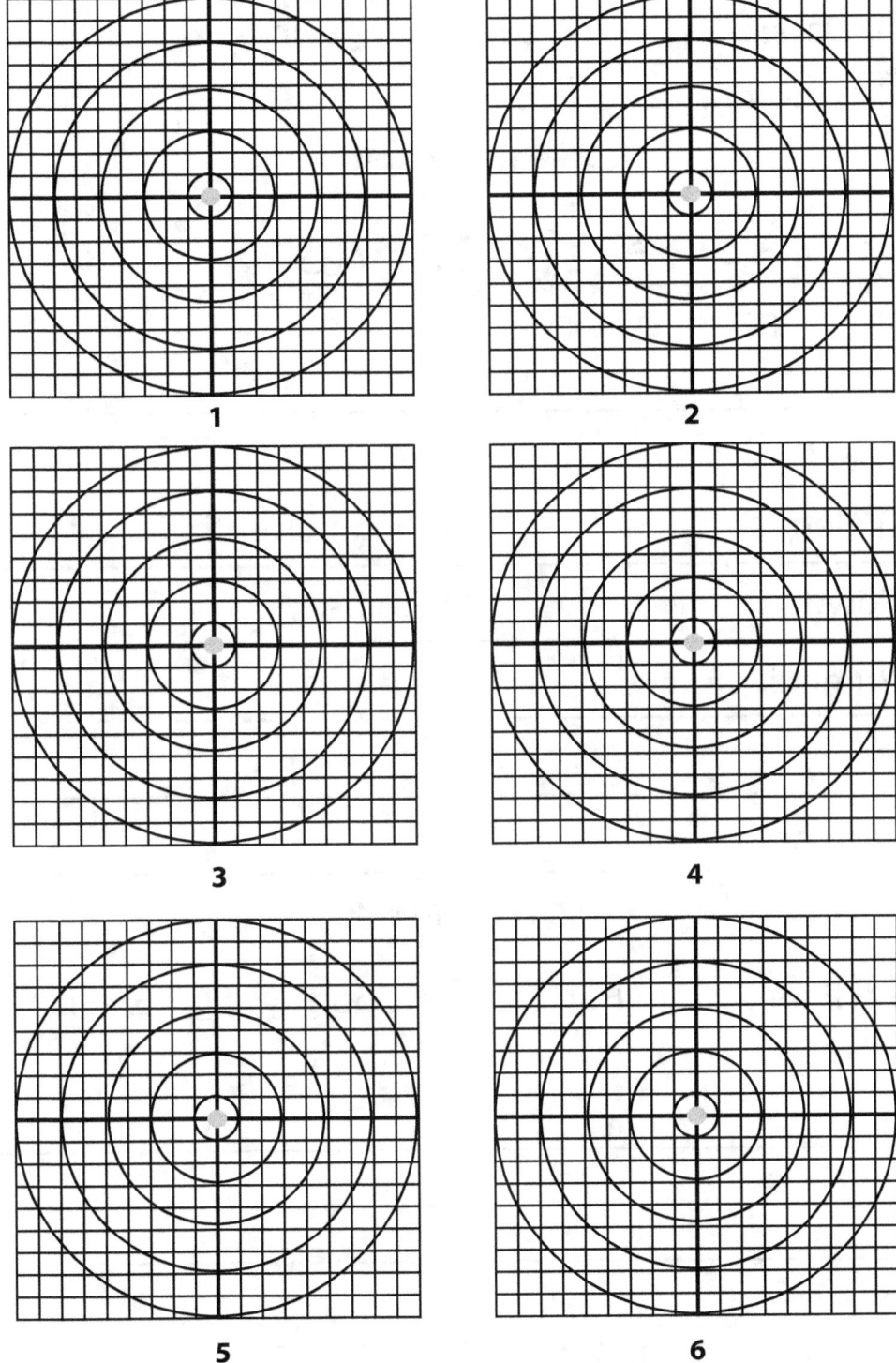

Date: _____ Time: _____

Location: _____

Weather Conditions

☀ ☁ ⛅ 🌧 🌨 🌨 🚩 🌡
☐ ☐ ☐ ☐ ☐ ☐

Firearm:	
Bullet:	Seating Depth:
Powder:	Grains:
Primer:	
Brass:	
Distance:	

Overall Results

☐ Poor   ☐ Fair   ☐ Good   ☐ Excellent

Notes

_____
_____
_____

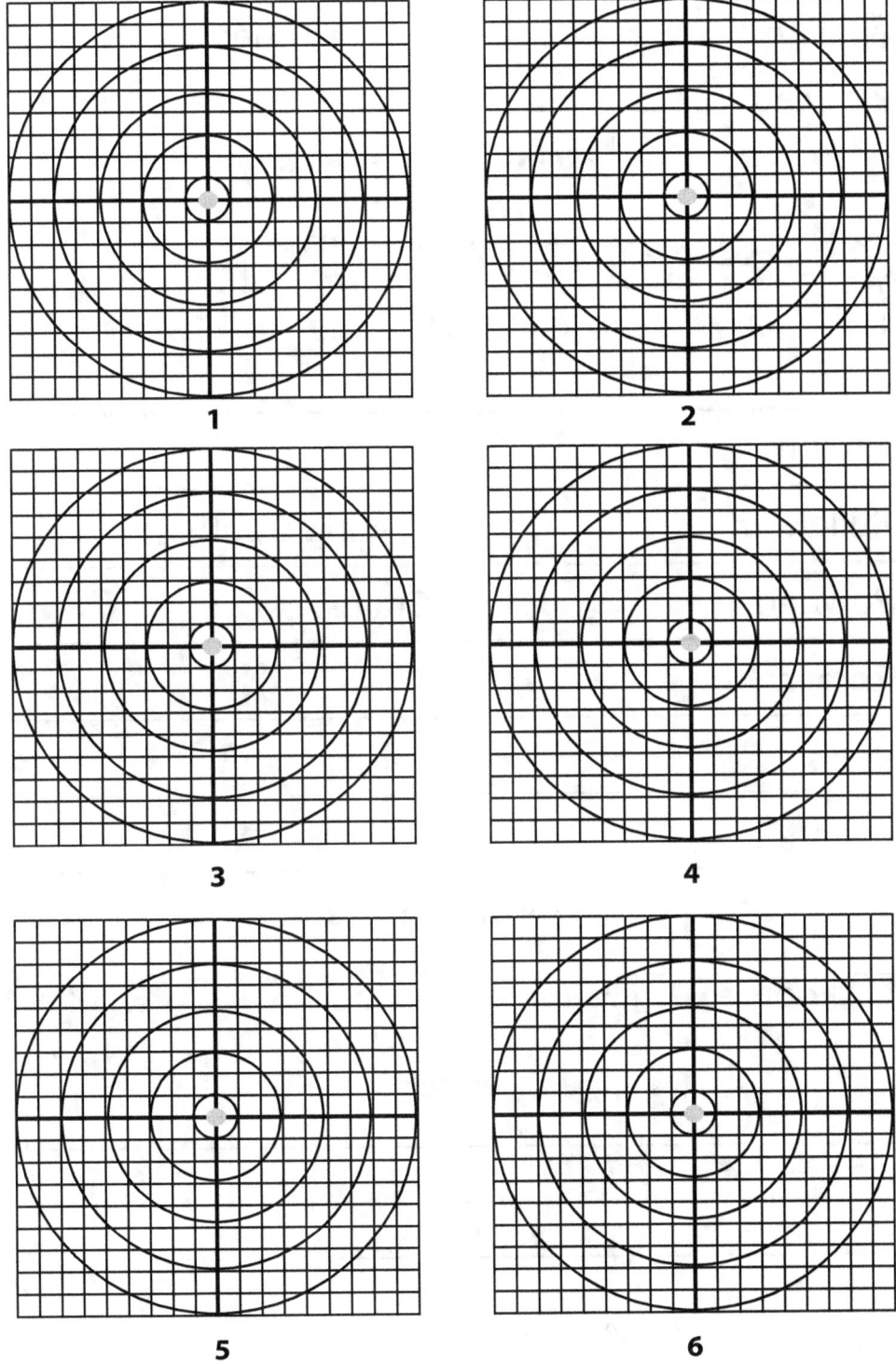

Date: _____   Time: _____
Location: _____

Weather Conditions

☀ ☁ ⛅ 🌧 🌧 🌨 🚩 🌡
☐ ☐ ☐ ☐ ☐ ☐ ___ ___

Firearm:	
Bullet:	Seating Depth:
Powder:	Grains:
Primer:	
Brass:	
Distance:	

Overall Results

☐ Poor   ☐ Fair   ☐ Good   ☐ Excellent

Notes

_____
_____
_____

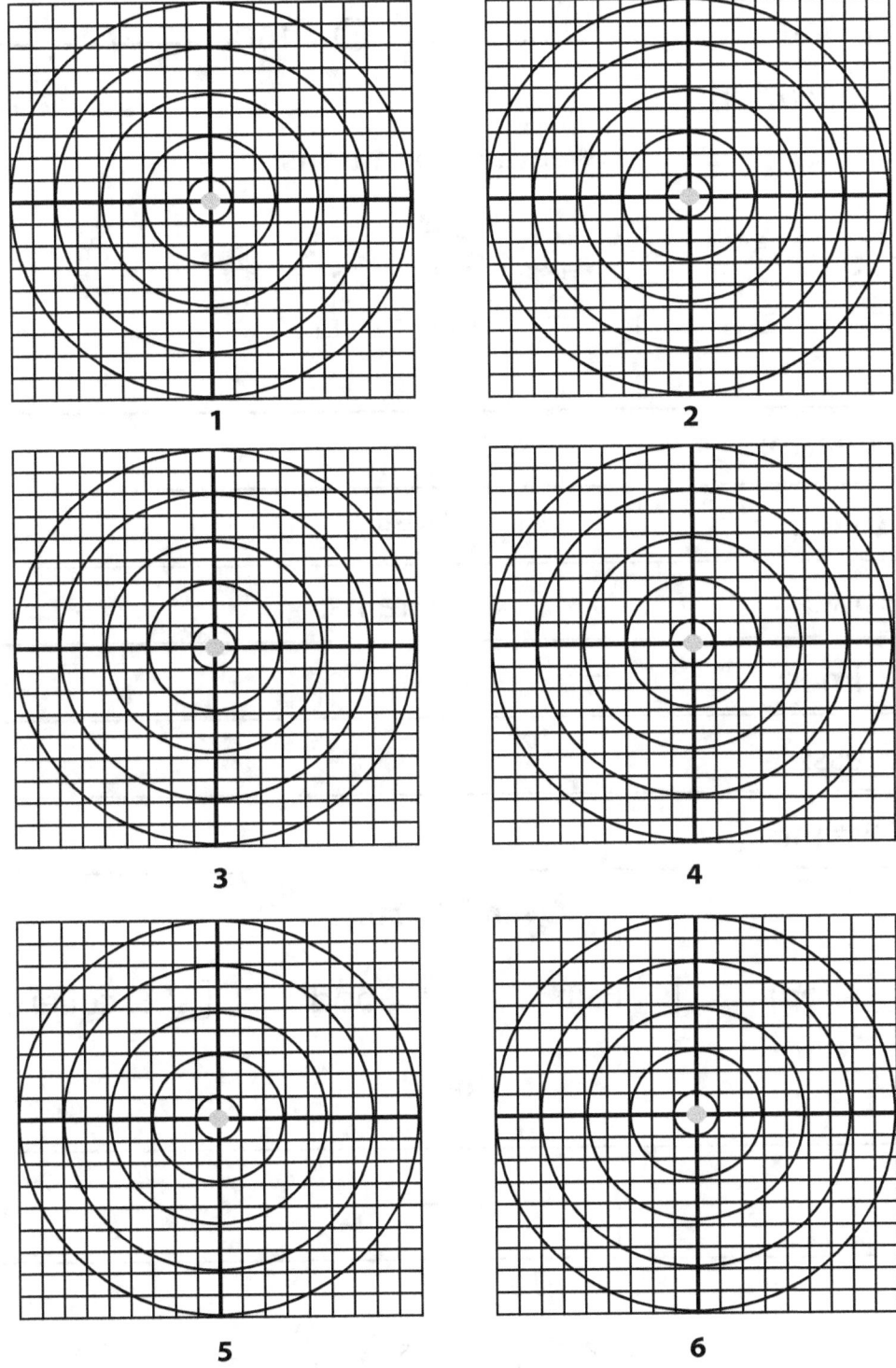

📅 Date: _____ 🕐 Time: _____

📍 Location: _____

Weather Conditions

☀️ ☐   ⛅ ☐   🌥️ ☐   🌦️ ☐   🌧️ ☐   🌨️ ☐   🚩 _____   🌡️

Firearm:	
Bullet:	Seating Depth:
Powder:	Grains:
Primer:	
Brass:	
Distance:	

Overall Results

☐ Poor   ☐ Fair   ☐ Good   ☐ Excellent

Notes

_____

_____

_____

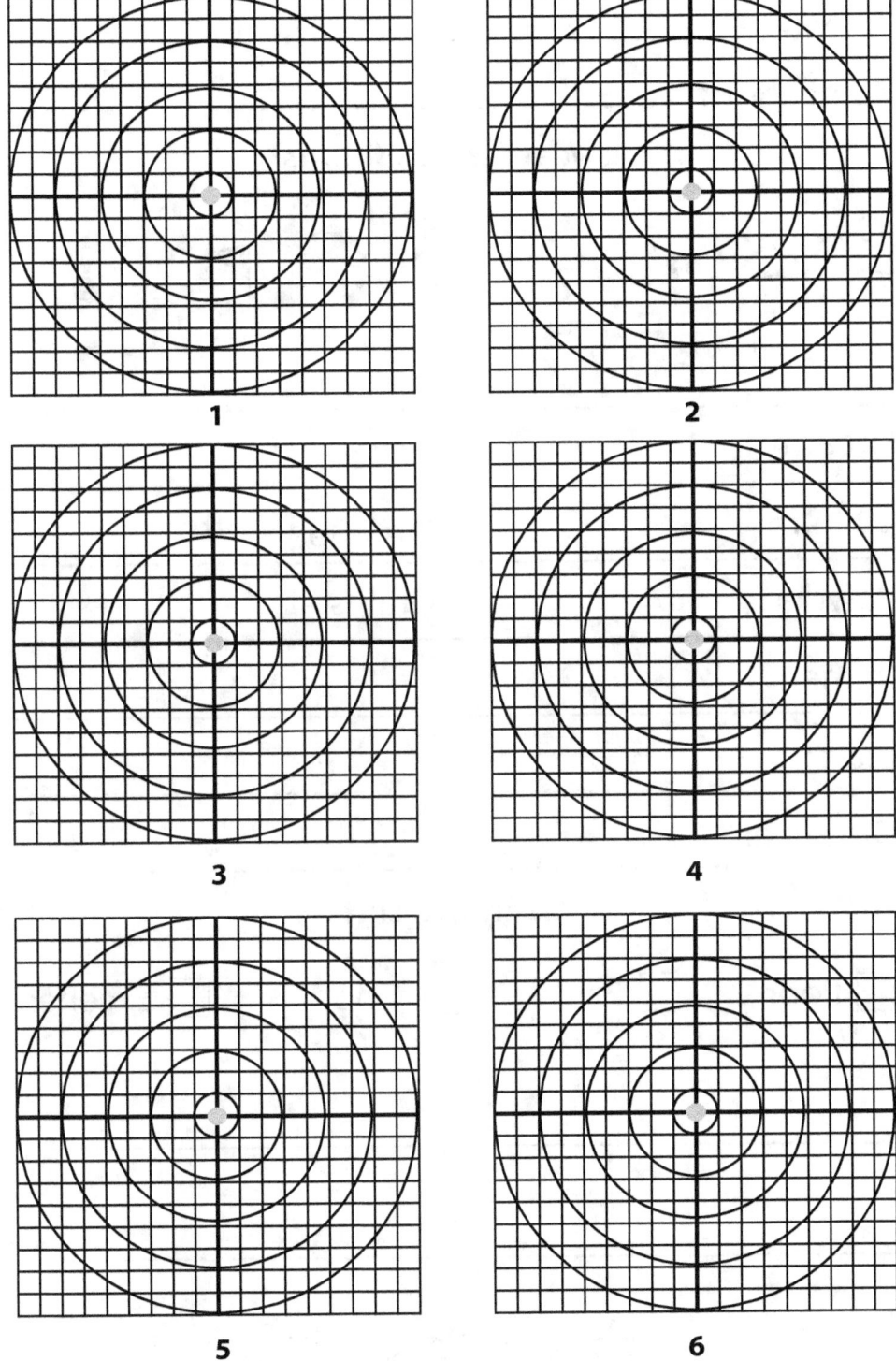

Date: _____ Time: _____

Location: _____

Weather Conditions

☀ ☁ ⛅ 🌧 🌦 ❄ 🚩 🌡
☐ ☐ ☐ ☐ ☐ ☐   _____

Firearm:	
Bullet:	Seating Depth:
Powder:	Grains:
Primer:	
Brass:	
Distance:	

Overall Results

☐ Poor   ☐ Fair   ☐ Good   ☐ Excellent

Notes

_____
_____
_____

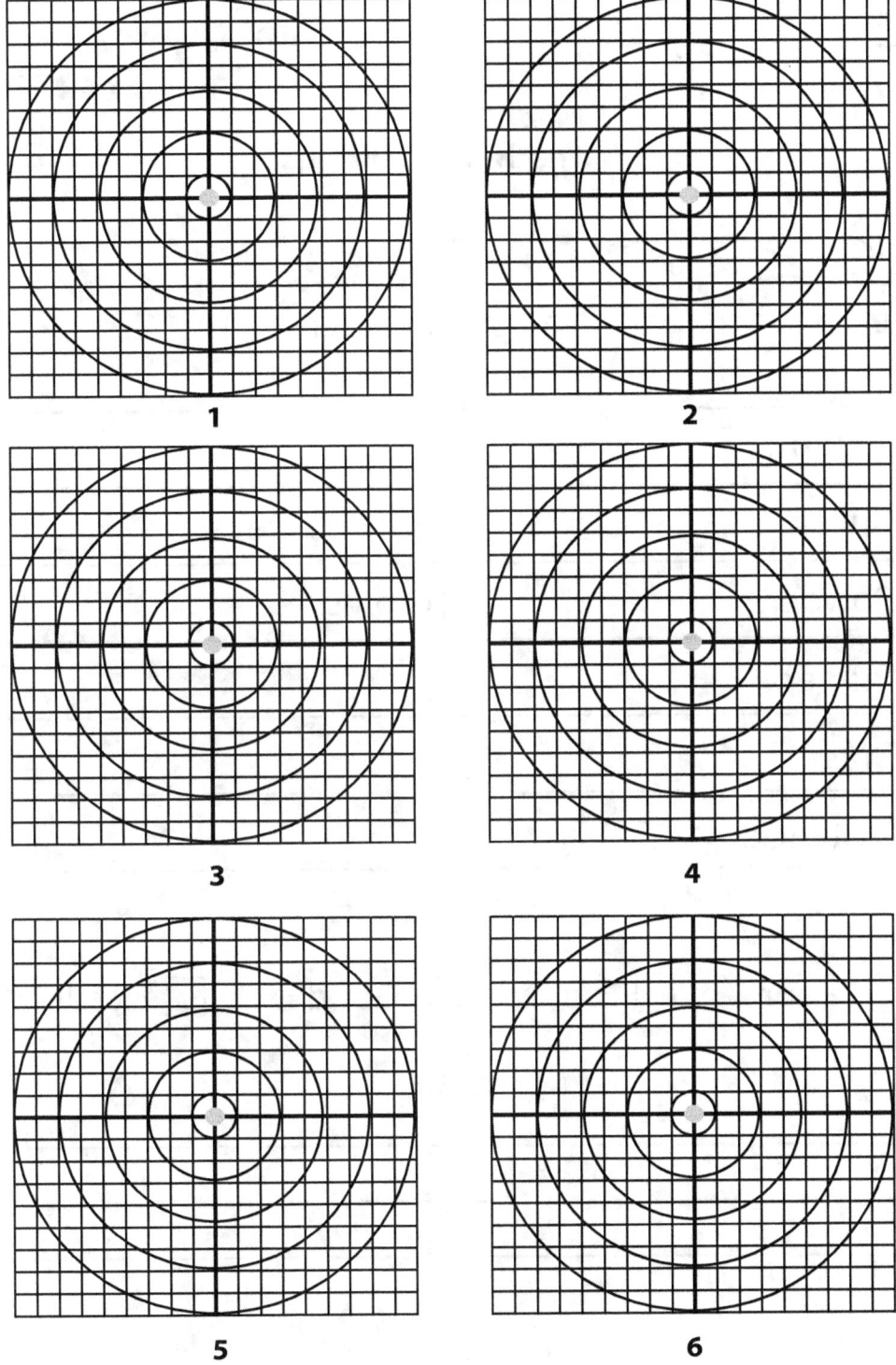

Date: _____ Time: _____

Location: _____

Weather Conditions

☀ ☁ ⛅ 🌧 🌧 🌨 🚩 🌡
☐ ☐ ☐ ☐ ☐ ☐

Firearm:	
Bullet:	Seating Depth:
Powder:	Grains:
Primer:	
Brass:	
Distance:	

Overall Results

☐ Poor ☐ Fair ☐ Good ☐ Excellent

Notes

_____
_____
_____

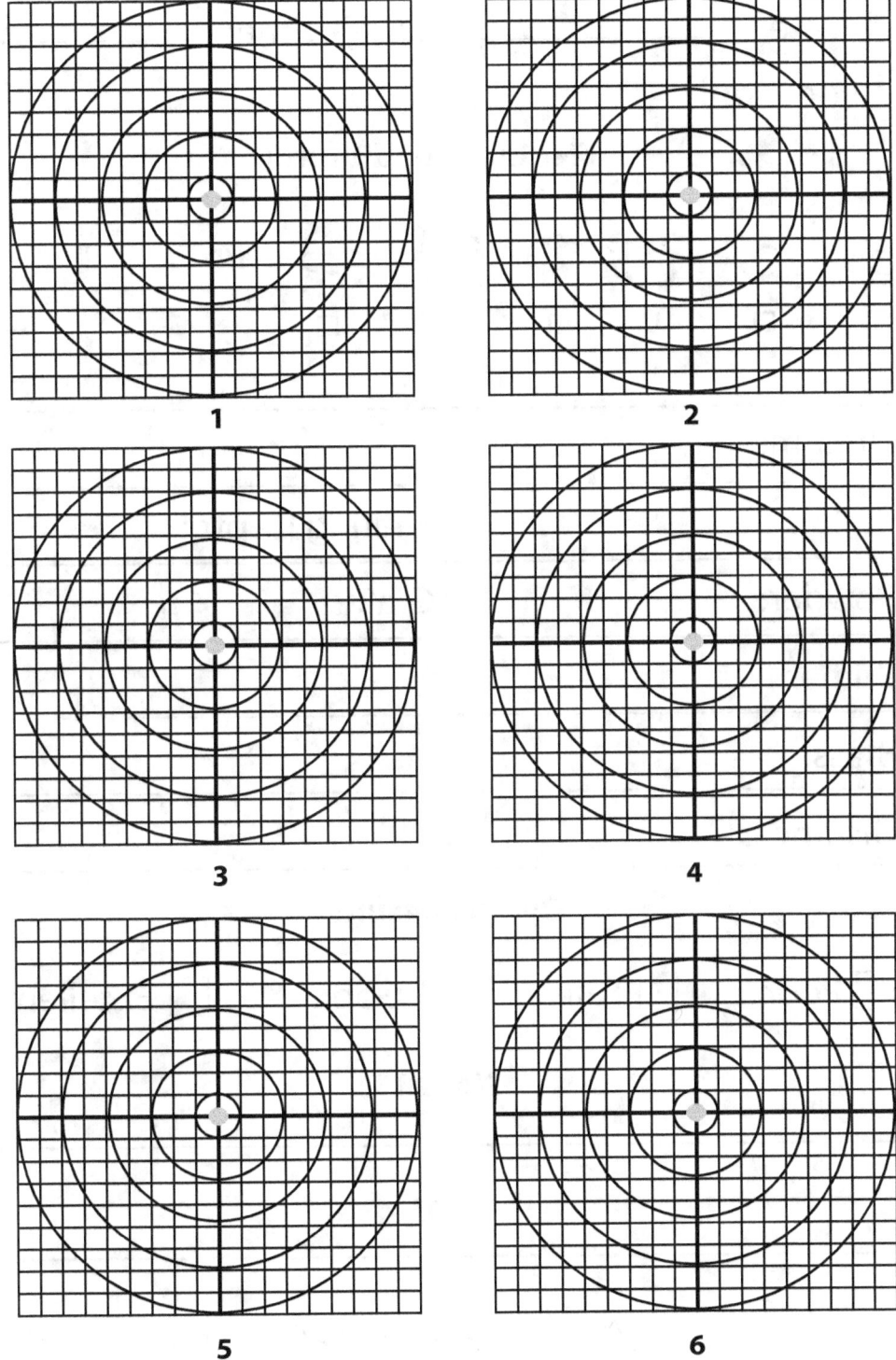

Date: _____   Time: _____

Location: _____

Weather Conditions

☀ ☁ ⛅ 🌧 🌧 🌨 🚩 🌡
☐   ☐   ☐   ☐   ☐   ☐   ☐

Firearm:	
Bullet:	Seating Depth:
Powder:	Grains:
Primer:	
Brass:	
Distance:	

Overall Results

☐ Poor   ☐ Fair   ☐ Good   ☐ Excellent

Notes

_____
_____
_____

☆ ☆ ☆ ☆ ☆

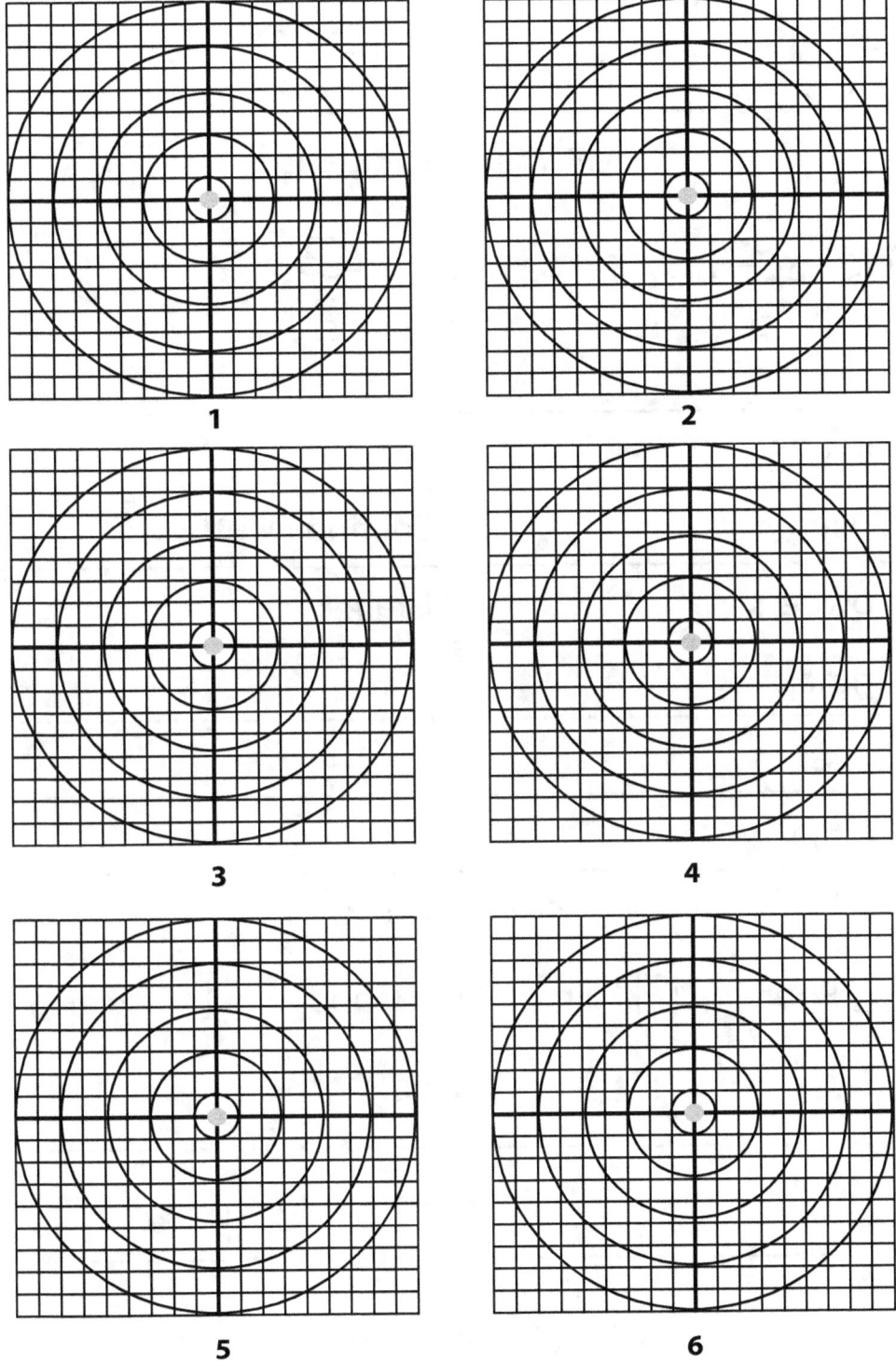

📅 Date: _____ 🕐 Time: _____
📍 Location: _____

Weather Conditions

☀️ ☁️ ⛅ 🌥️ 🌧️ 🌨️ 🚩 🌡️
☐   ☐   ☐   ☐   ☐   ☐

Firearm:	
Bullet:	Seating Depth:
Powder:	Grains:
Primer:	
Brass:	
Distance:	

Overall Results

☐ Poor   ☐ Fair   ☐ Good   ☐ Excellent

Notes

_____
_____
_____

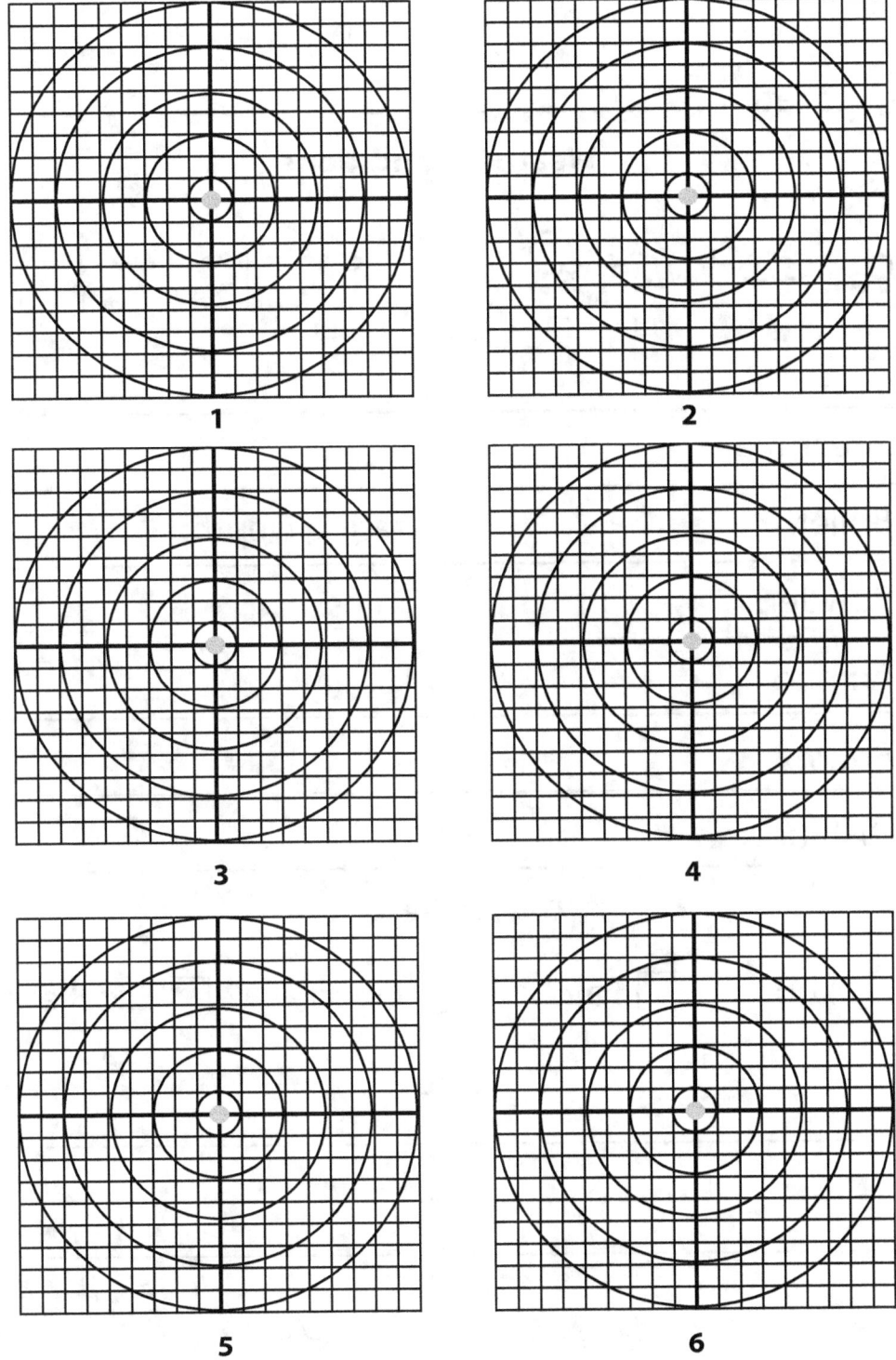

Date: _____ Time: _____

Location: _____

Weather Conditions

☀ ☐   ☁ ☐   ⛅ ☐   🌧 ☐   🌧 ☐   🌨 ☐   🚩 _____   🌡 _____

Firearm:	
Bullet:	Seating Depth:
Powder:	Grains:
Primer:	
Brass:	
Distance:	

Overall Results

☐ Poor   ☐ Fair   ☐ Good   ☐ Excellent

Notes

_____
_____
_____

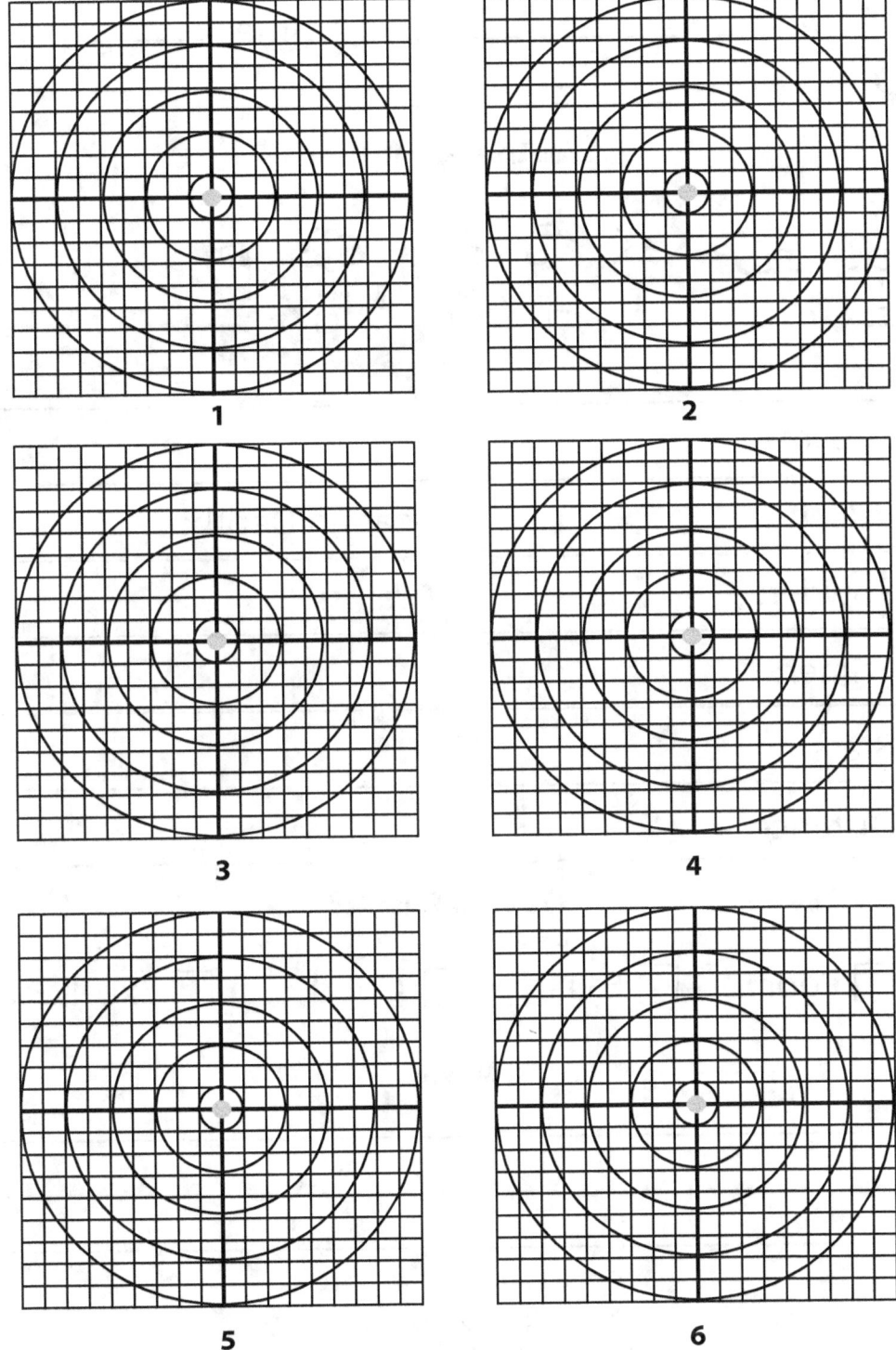

📅 Date: _____ 🕐 Time: _____
📍 Location: _____

Weather Conditions

☀ ☁ ⛅ 🌧 🌧 🌨 🚩 🌡
☐ ☐ ☐ ☐ ☐ ☐ _____ _____

Firearm:	
Bullet:	Seating Depth:
Powder:	Grains:
Primer:	
Brass:	
Distance:	

Overall Results

☐ Poor   ☐ Fair   ☐ Good   ☐ Excellent

Notes

_____
_____
_____

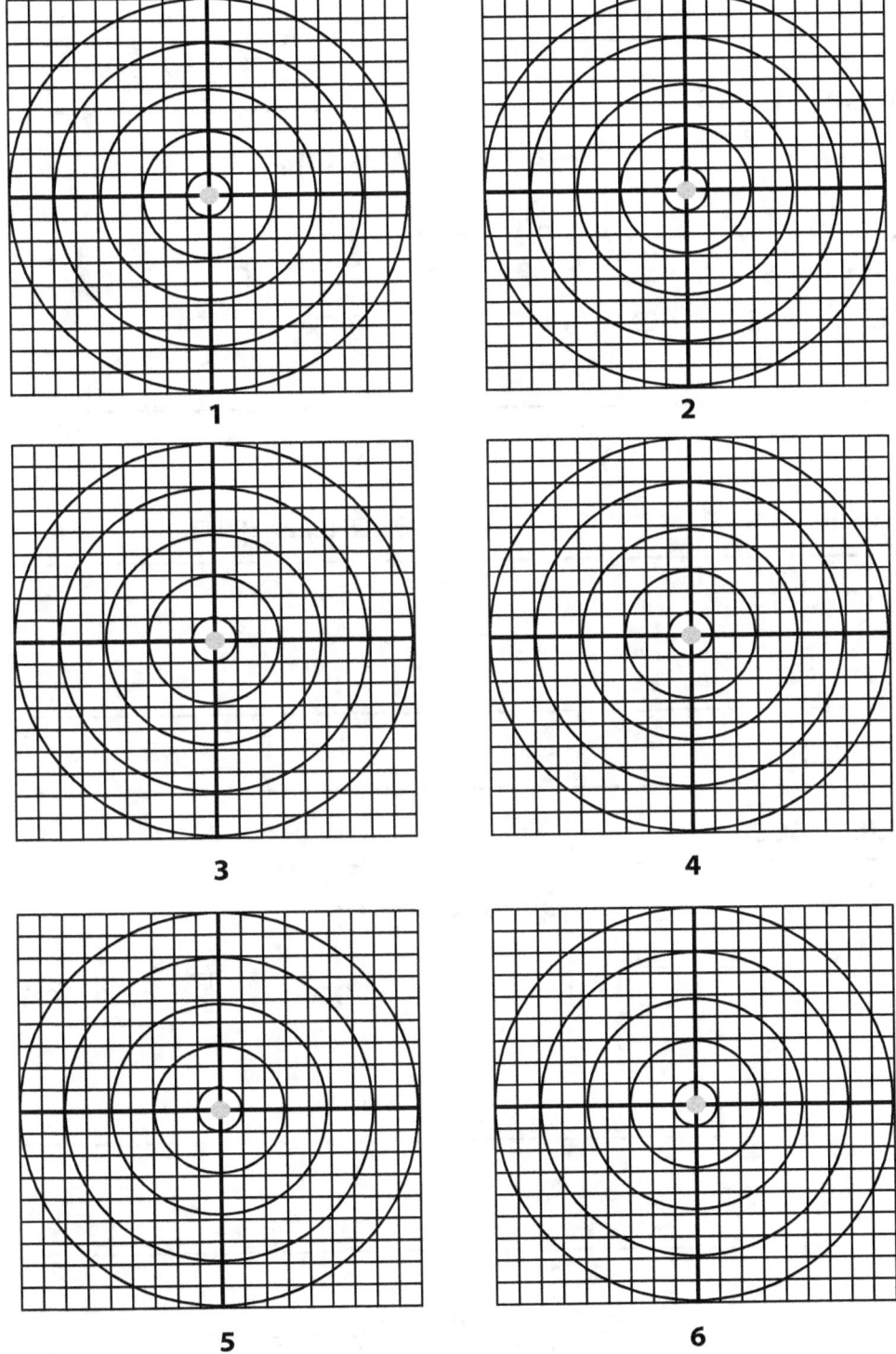

📅 Date: _____ 🕐 Time: _____

📍 Location: _____

Weather Conditions

☀️ ☐   ☁️ ☐   ⛅ ☐   🌧️ ☐   🌨️ ☐   ❄️ ☐   🚩   🌡️

Firearm:	
Bullet:	Seating Depth:
Powder:	Grains:
Primer:	
Brass:	
Distance:	

Overall Results

☐ Poor   ☐ Fair   ☐ Good   ☐ Excellent

Notes

_____

_____

_____

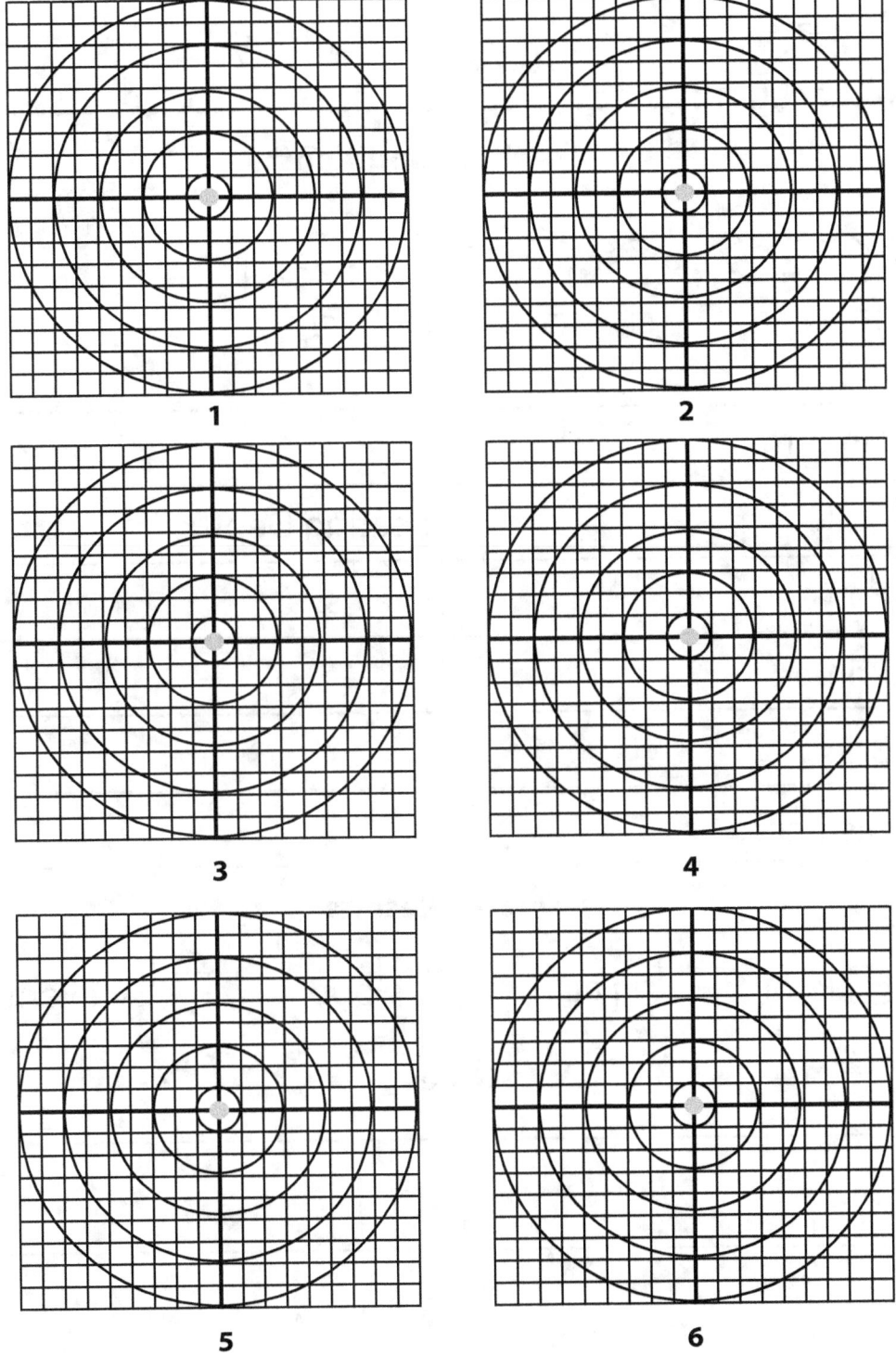

📅 Date: _____ 🕐 Time: _____

📍 Location: _____

Weather Conditions

☀️ ☁️ ⛅ 🌧️ 🌧️ 🌨️ 🚩 🌡️
☐   ☐   ☐   ☐   ☐   ☐

Firearm:	
Bullet:	Seating Depth:
Powder:	Grains:
Primer:	
Brass:	
Distance:	

Overall Results

☐ Poor   ☐ Fair   ☐ Good   ☐ Excellent

Notes

_____

_____

_____

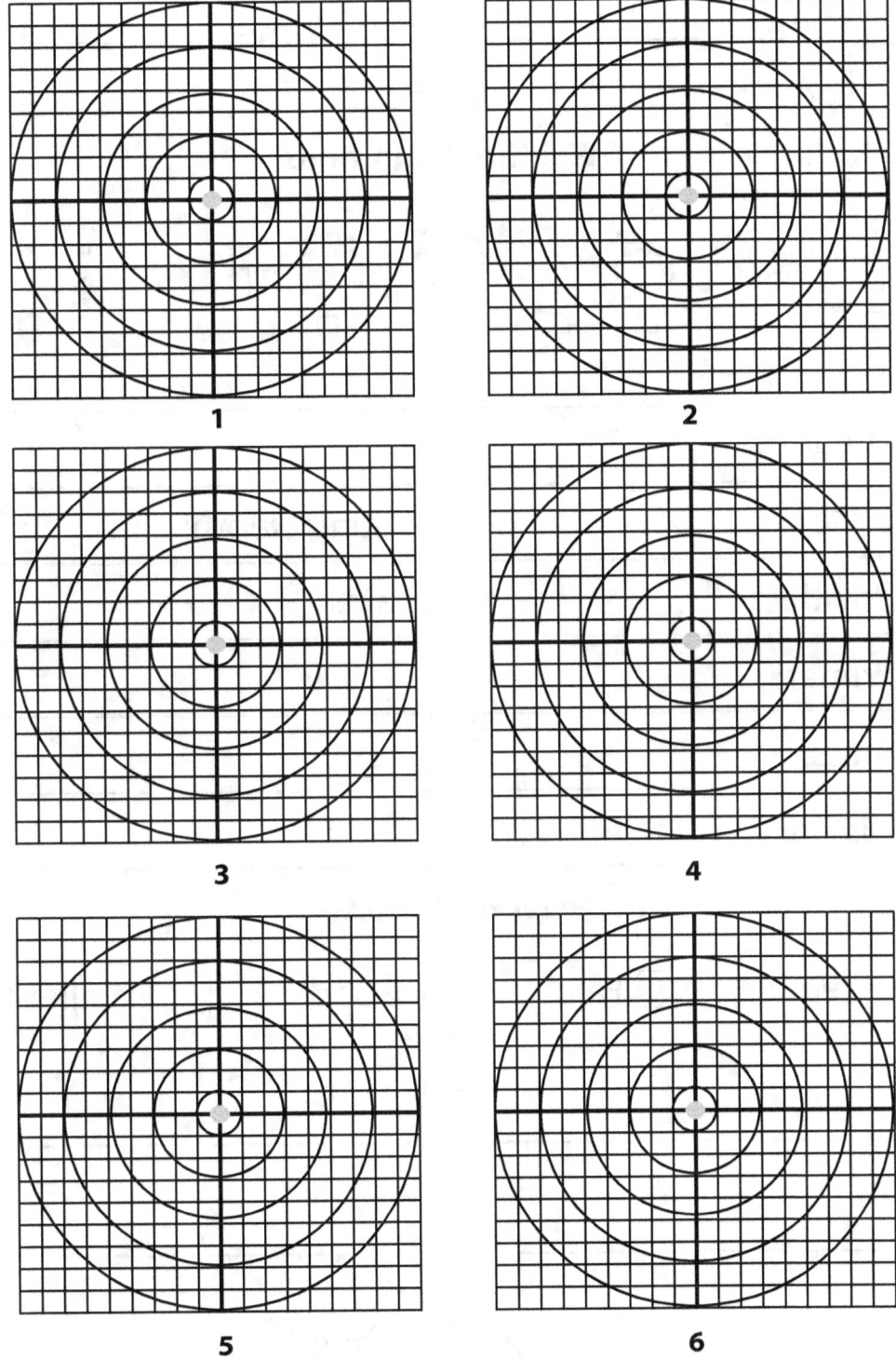

📅 Date: _____ 🕐 Time: _____

📍 Location: _____

Weather Conditions

☀️ ☐   ☁️ ☐   🌤️ ☐   🌧️ ☐   🌦️ ☐   🌨️ ☐   🚩 _____   🌡️ _____

Firearm:	
Bullet:	Seating Depth:
Powder:	Grains:
Primer:	
Brass:	
Distance:	

Overall Results

☐ Poor   ☐ Fair   ☐ Good   ☐ Excellent

Notes

_____

_____

_____

☆ ☆ ☆ ☆ ☆

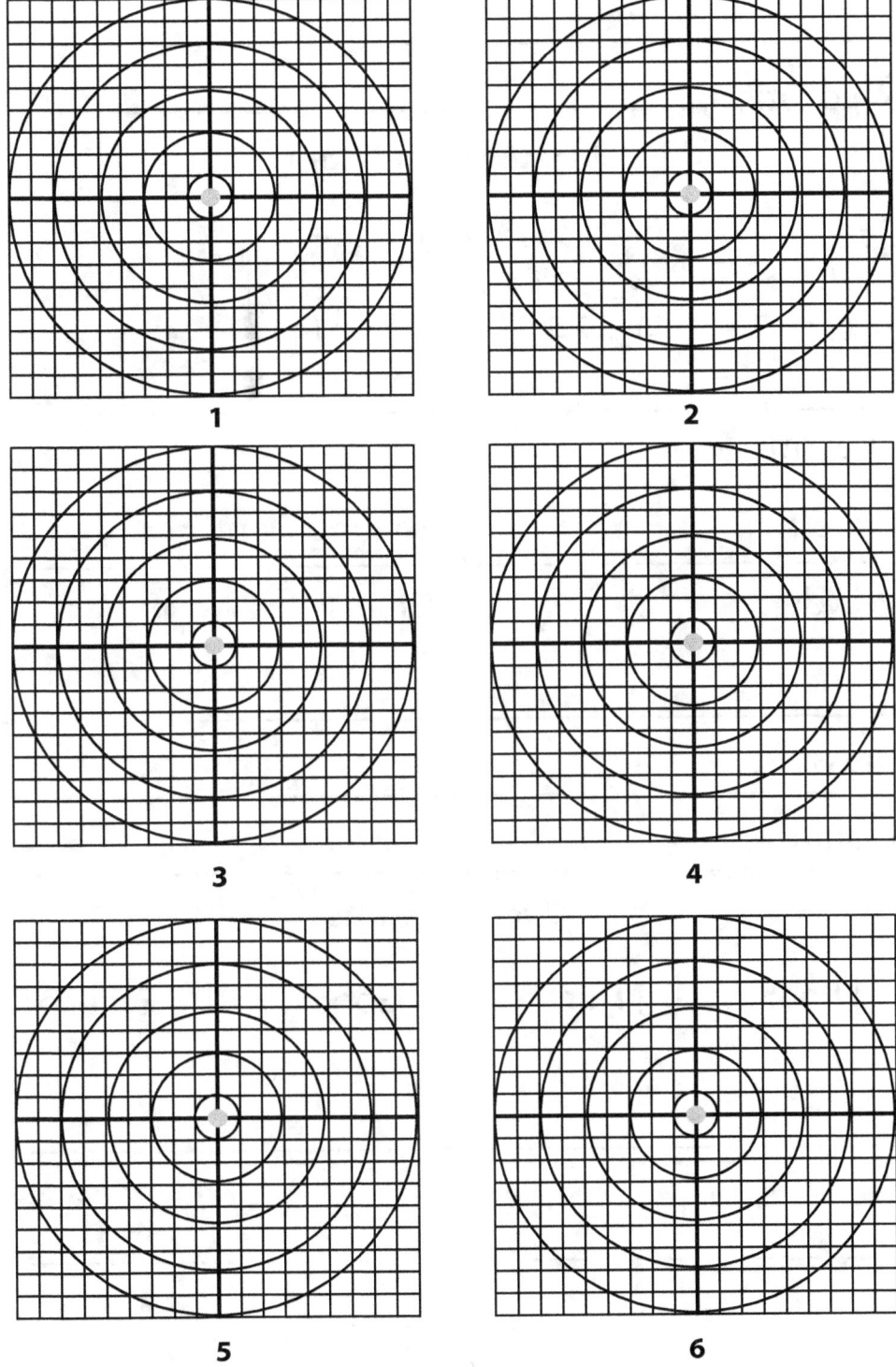

Date: _____ Time: _____

 Location: _____

Weather Conditions

☀ ☁ ⛅ 🌧 🌧 🌨 🚩 🌡
☐   ☐   ☐   ☐   ☐   ☐   _____ _____

Firearm:	
Bullet:	Seating Depth:
Powder:	Grains:
Primer:	
Brass:	
Distance:	

Overall Results

☐ Poor   ☐ Fair   ☐ Good   ☐ Excellent

Notes

_____
_____
_____

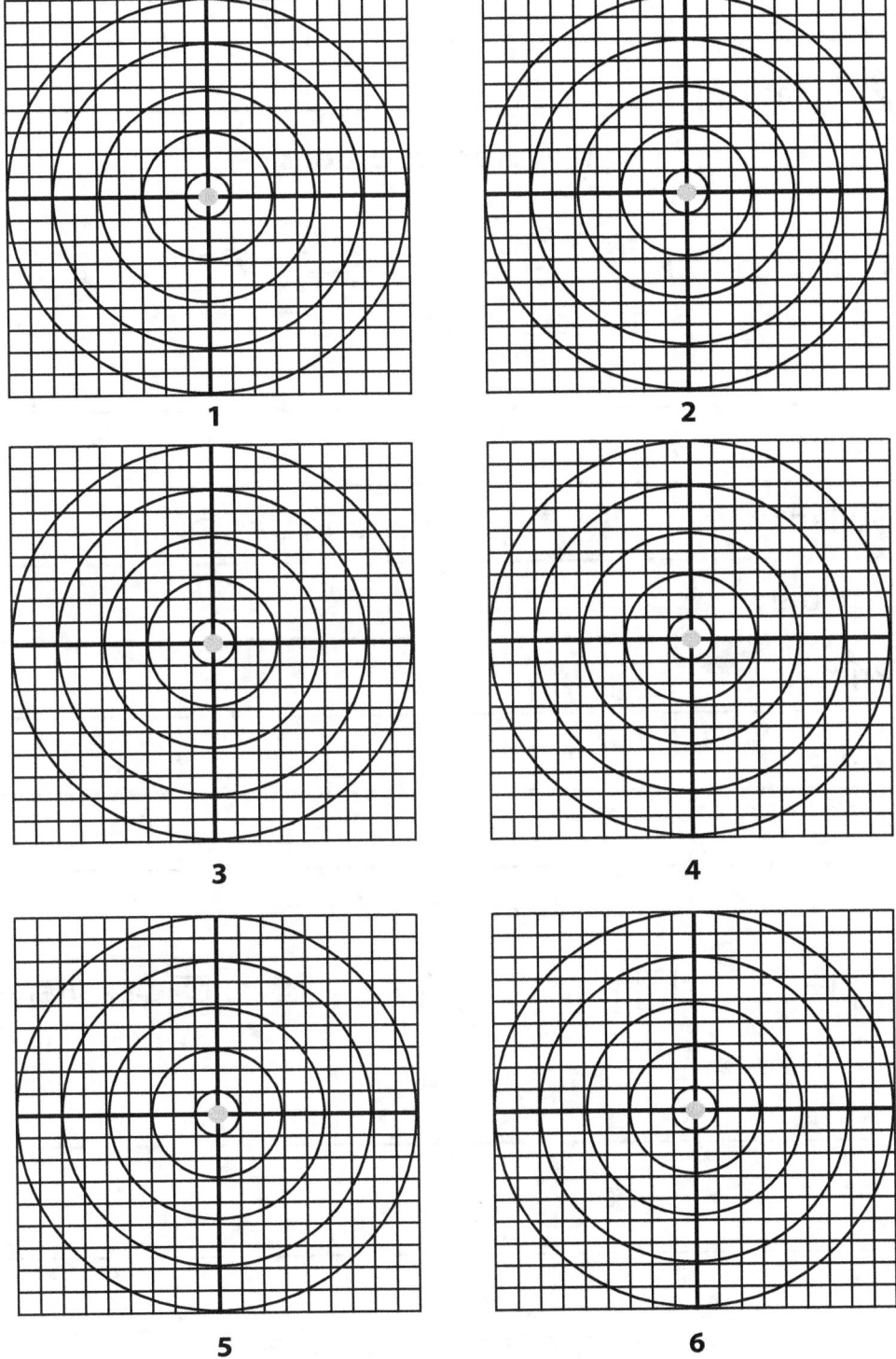

📅 Date: _____ 🕐 Time: _____

📍 Location: _____

Weather Conditions

☀ ☁ ⛅ 🌧 🌦 🌨 🚩 🌡
☐ ☐ ☐ ☐ ☐ ☐

Firearm:	
Bullet:	Seating Depth:
Powder:	Grains:
Primer:	
Brass:	
Distance:	

Overall Results

☐ Poor ☐ Fair ☐ Good ☐ Excellent

Notes

_____
_____
_____

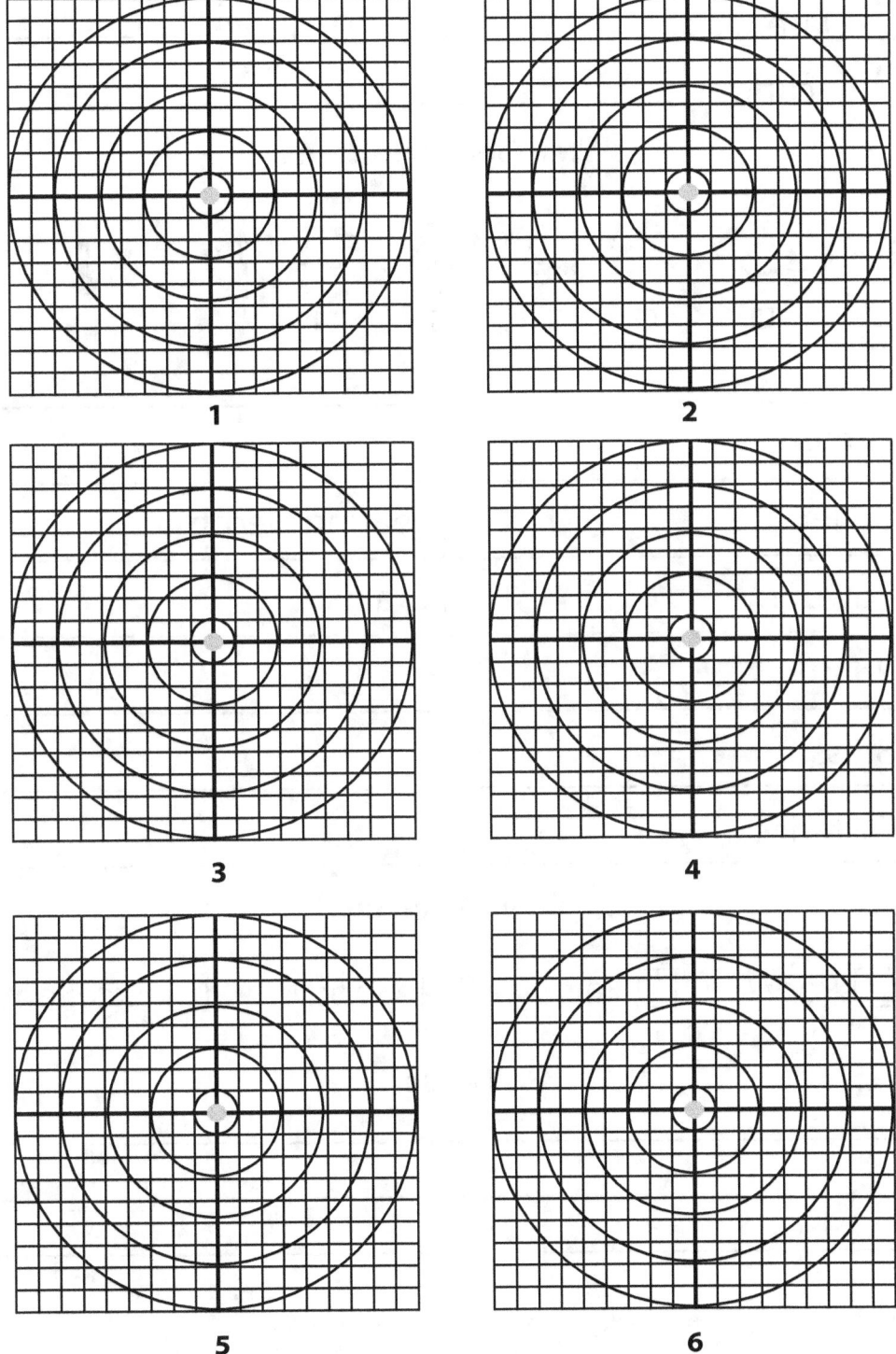

Date: _____ Time: _____

 Location: _____

Weather Conditions

☀ ☁ ⛅ 🌧 🌦 🌨 🚩 🌡
☐   ☐   ☐   ☐   ☐   ☐   _____   _____

Firearm:	
Bullet:	Seating Depth:
Powder:	Grains:
Primer:	
Brass:	
Distance:	

Overall Results

☐ Poor   ☐ Fair   ☐ Good   ☐ Excellent

Notes

_____
_____
_____

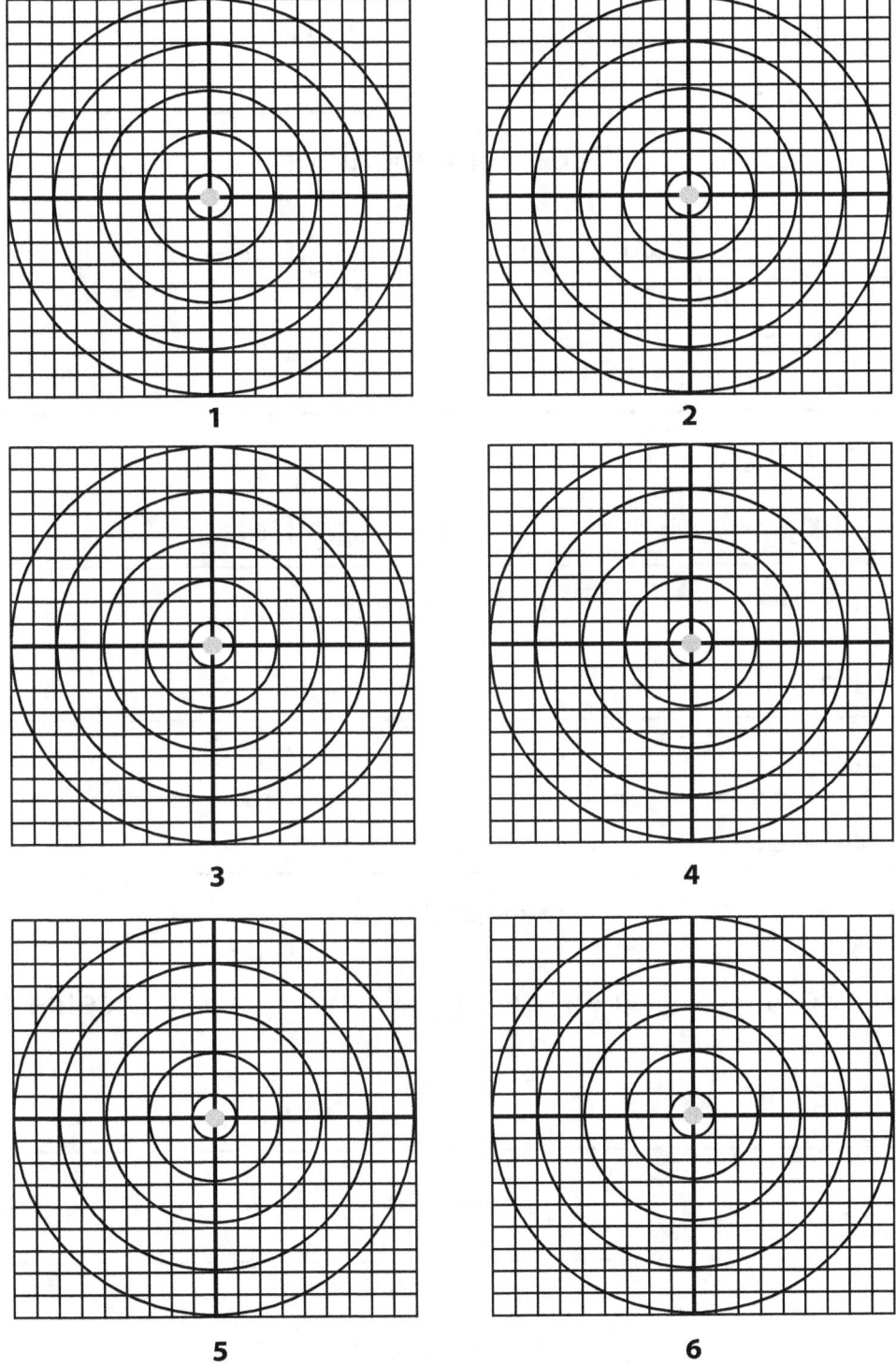

🗓 Date: _____ 🕐 Time: _____

📍 Location: _____

Weather Conditions

☀ ☁ ⛅ 🌥 🌧 🌨 🚩 🌡
☐ ☐ ☐ ☐ ☐ ☐ _____ _____

Firearm:	
Bullet:	Seating Depth:
Powder:	Grains:
Primer:	
Brass:	
Distance:	

Overall Results

☐ Poor   ☐ Fair   ☐ Good   ☐ Excellent

Notes

_____
_____
_____

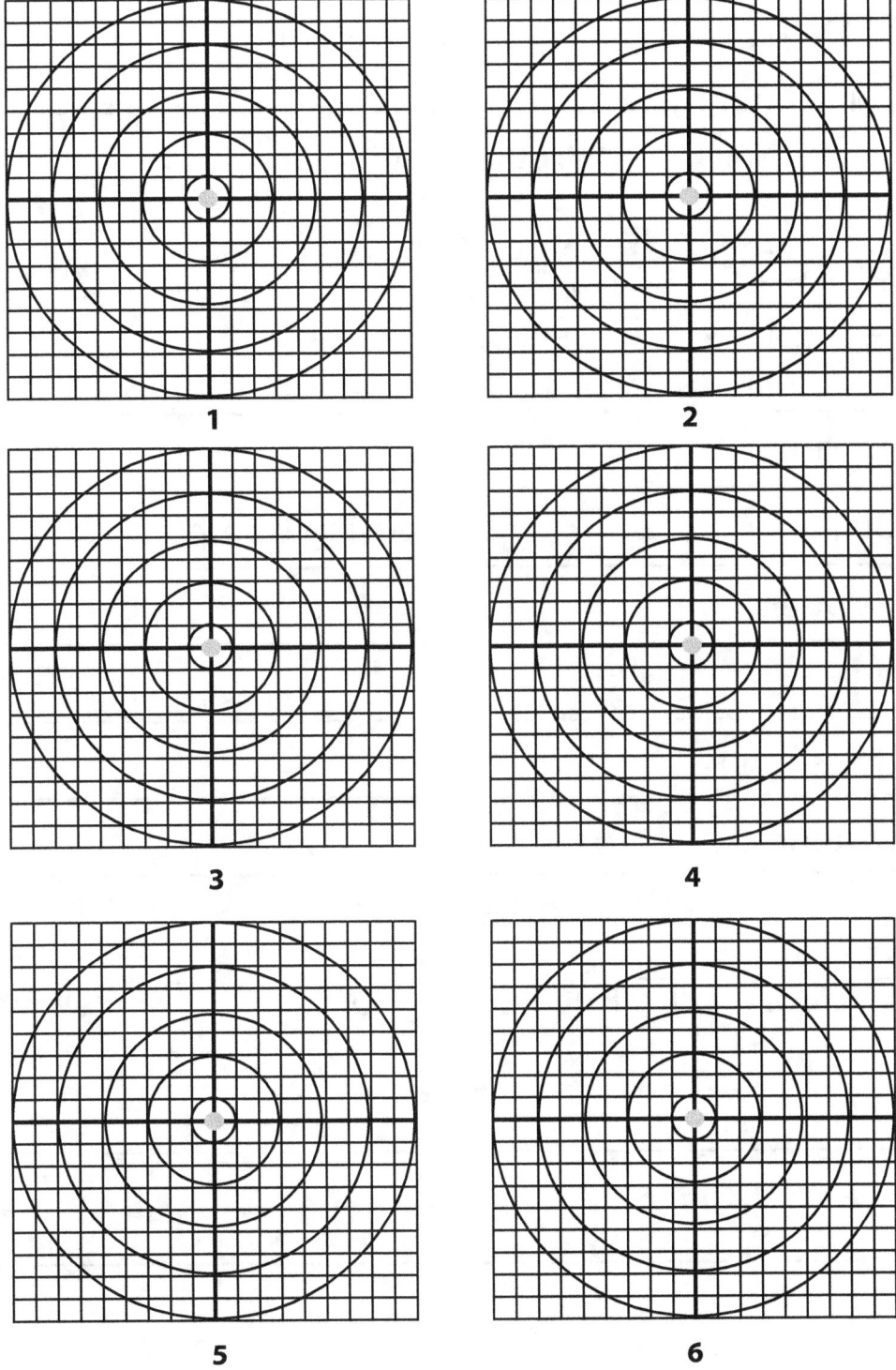

Date: _____ **Time:** _____

Location: _____

Weather Conditions

☀ ☁ ⛅ 🌧 🌧 🌨 🚩 🌡
☐ ☐ ☐ ☐ ☐ ☐

Firearm:	
Bullet:	Seating Depth:
Powder:	Grains:
Primer:	
Brass:	
Distance:	

Overall Results

☐ Poor ☐ Fair ☐ Good ☐ Excellent

Notes

_____
_____
_____

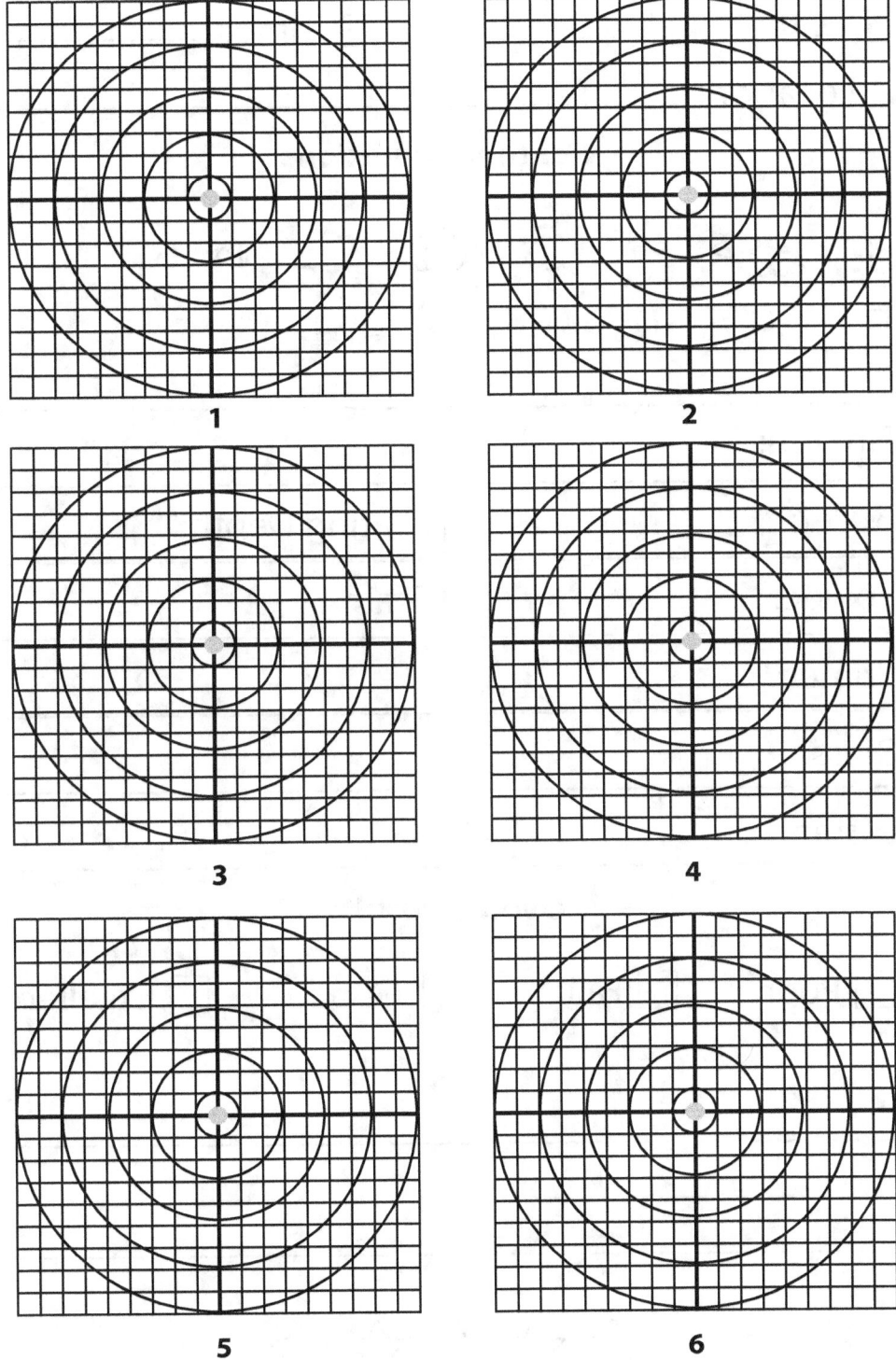

Date: _____   Time: _____

 Location: _____

Weather Conditions

☀ ☁ ⛅ 🌧 🌨 ❄ 🚩 🌡
☐ ☐ ☐ ☐ ☐ ☐

Firearm:	
Bullet:	Seating Depth:
Powder:	Grains:
Primer:	
Brass:	
Distance:	

Overall Results

☐ Poor   ☐ Fair   ☐ Good   ☐ Excellent

Notes

_____
_____
_____

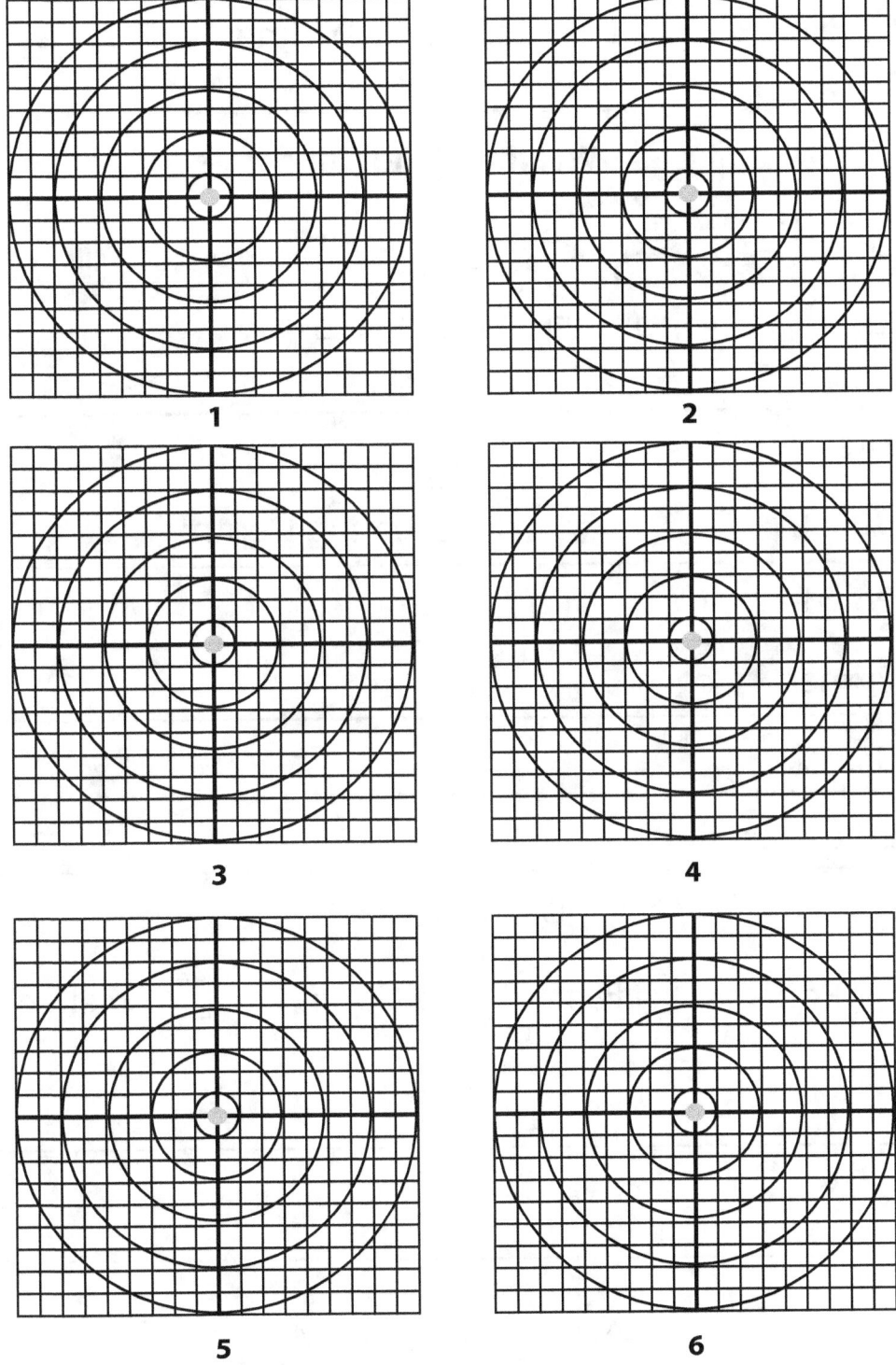

Date: _____   🕐 Time: _____
📍 Location: _____

Weather Conditions

☀ ☁ ⛅ 🌧 🌧 🌨 🚩 _____   🌡
☐   ☐   ☐   ☐   ☐   ☐

Firearm:	
Bullet:	Seating Depth:
Powder:	Grains:
Primer:	
Brass:	
Distance:	

Overall Results

☐ Poor ☐ Fair ☐ Good ☐ Excellent

Notes

_____
_____
_____

☆ ☆ ☆ ☆ ☆

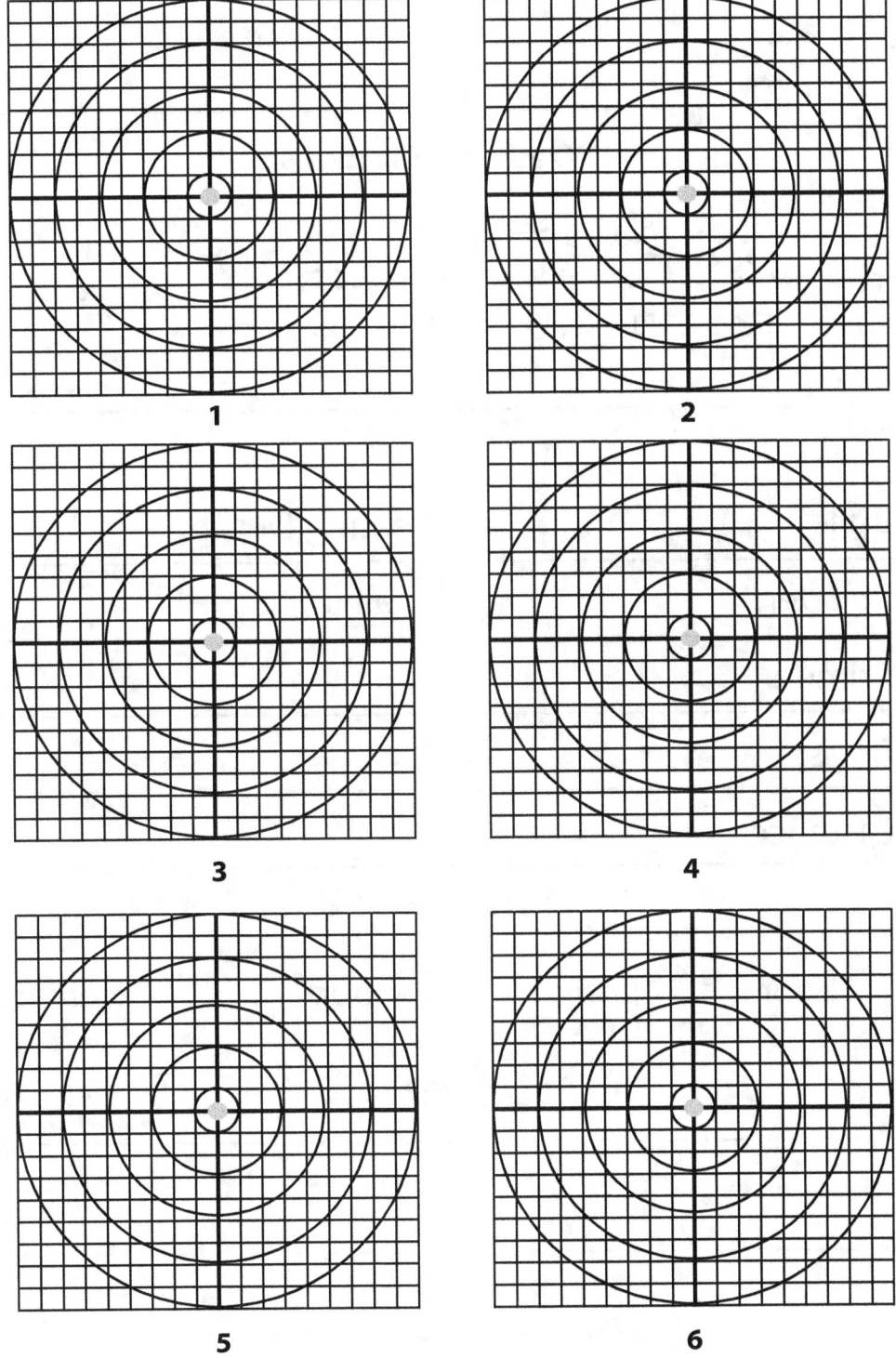

📅 Date: _____ 🕐 Time: _____

📍 Location: _____

Weather Conditions

☀ ☁ ⛅ 🌧 🌧 🌨 🚩 🌡
☐ ☐ ☐ ☐ ☐ ☐ _____

Firearm:	
Bullet:	Seating Depth:
Powder:	Grains:
Primer:	
Brass:	
Distance:	

Overall Results

☐ Poor   ☐ Fair   ☐ Good   ☐ Excellent

Notes

_____

_____

_____

☆ ☆ ☆ ☆ ☆

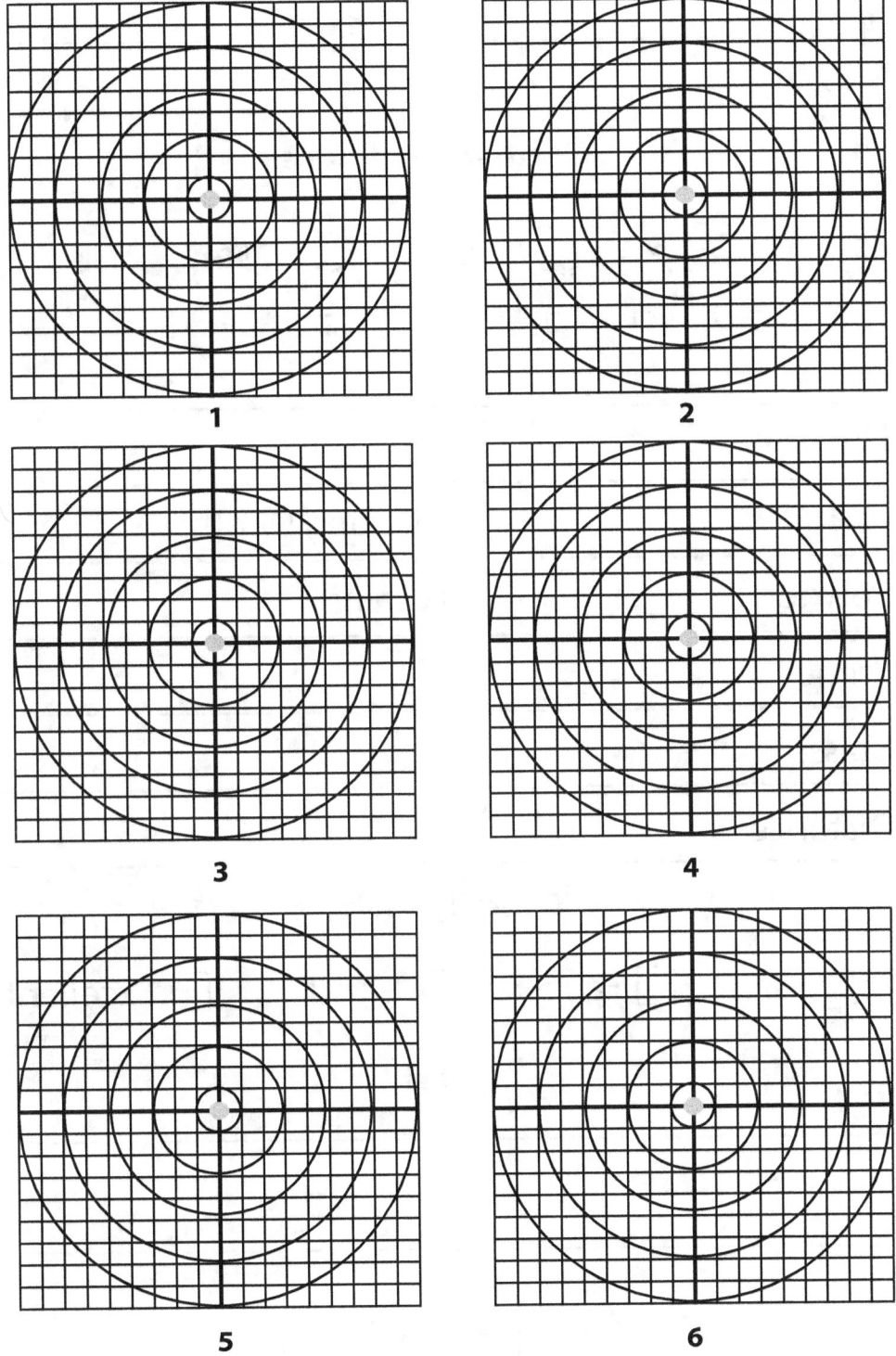

📅 Date: _____ 🕐 Time: _____

📍 Location: _____

Weather Conditions

☀️ ☐   ☁️ ☐   ⛅ ☐   🌦️ ☐   🌧️ ☐   🌨️ ☐   🚩 _____   🌡️ _____

Firearm:	
Bullet:	Seating Depth:
Powder:	Grains:
Primer:	
Brass:	
Distance:	

Overall Results

☐ Poor   ☐ Fair   ☐ Good   ☐ Excellent

Notes

_____
_____
_____

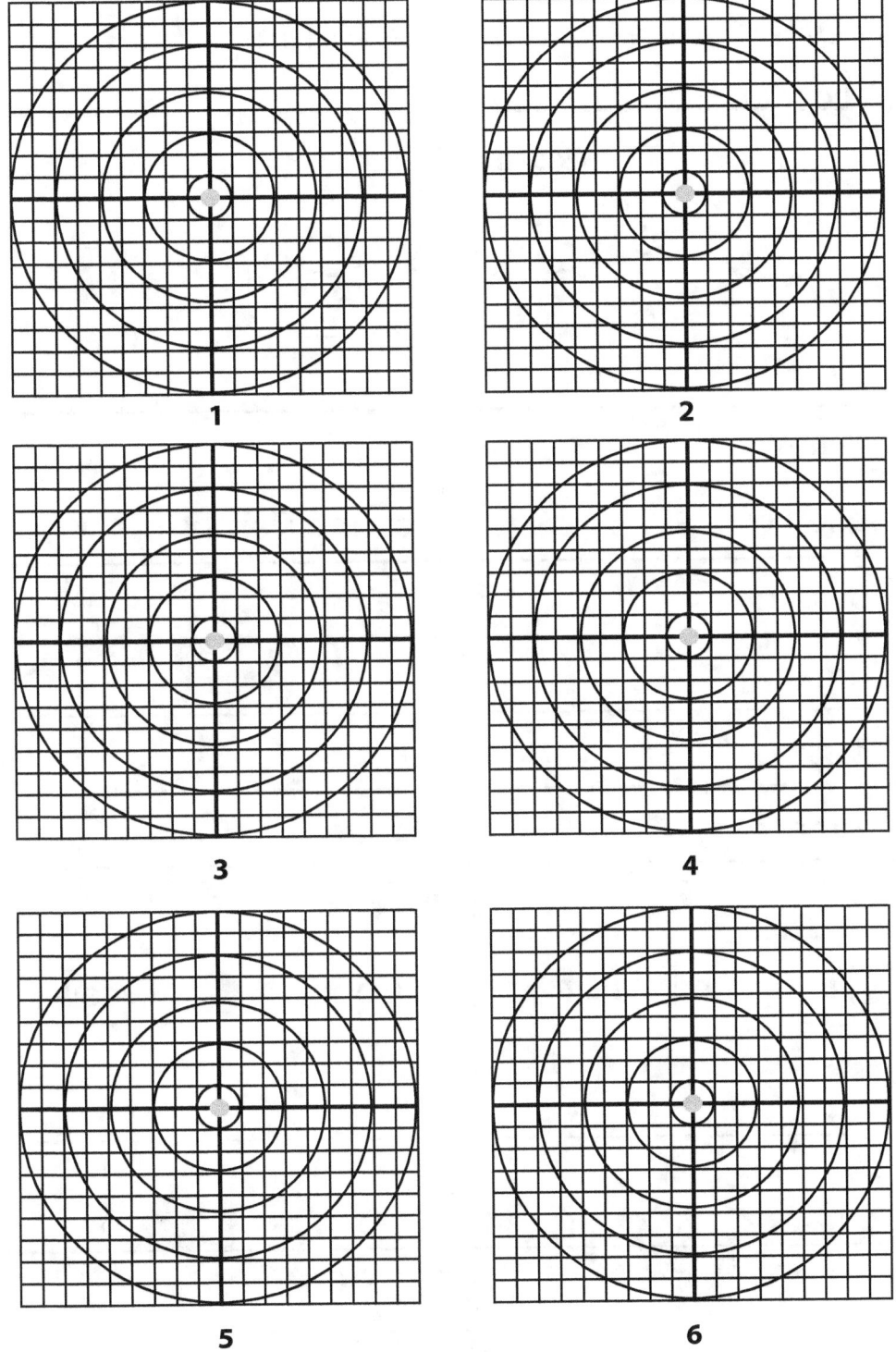

Date: _____ Time: _____
Location: _____

Weather Conditions

☀ ☁ ⛅ 🌧 🌧 ❄ 🚩 🌡
☐ ☐ ☐ ☐ ☐ ☐ ____ ____

Firearm:	
Bullet:	Seating Depth:
Powder:	Grains:
Primer:	
Brass:	
Distance:	

Overall Results

☐ Poor   ☐ Fair   ☐ Good   ☐ Excellent

Notes

_____
_____
_____

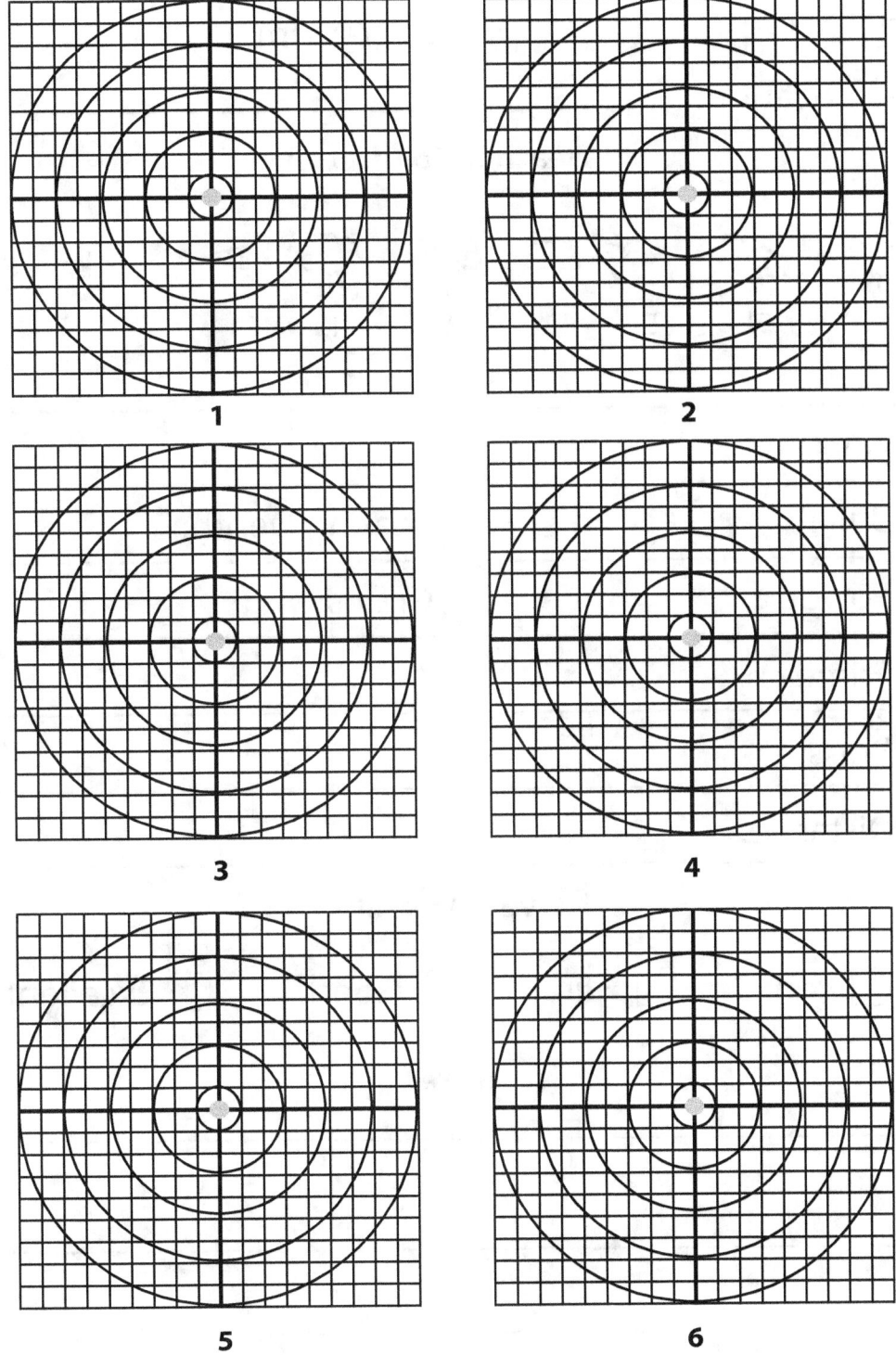

📅 Date: _____ 🕐 Time: _____

📍 Location: _____

Weather Conditions

☀ ☁ ⛅ 🌦 🌧 🌨 🚩 🌡
☐ ☐ ☐ ☐ ☐ ☐ ___ ___

Firearm:	
Bullet:	Seating Depth:
Powder:	Grains:
Primer:	
Brass:	
Distance:	

Overall Results

☐ Poor   ☐ Fair   ☐ Good   ☐ Excellent

Notes

_____
_____
_____

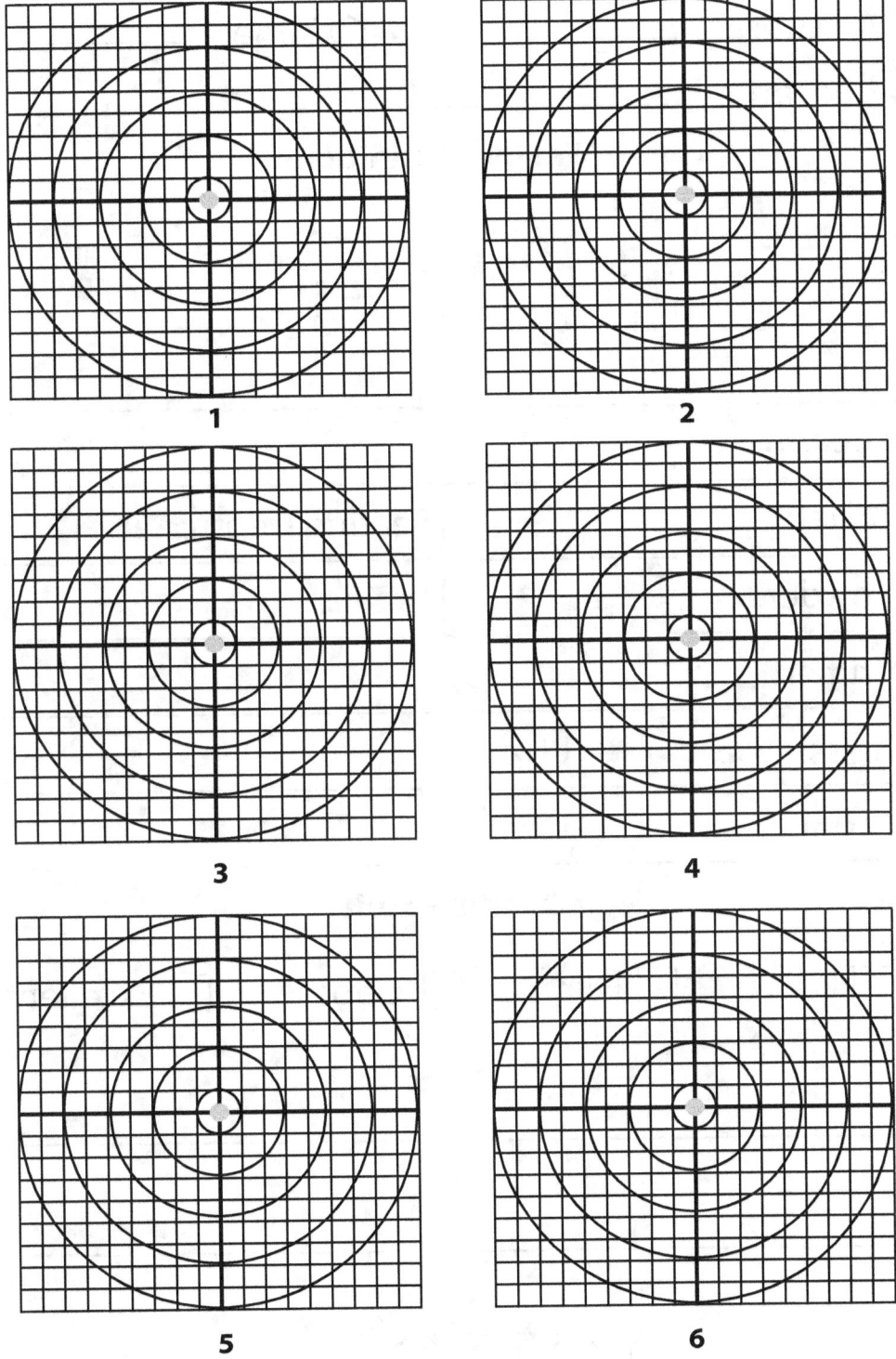

📅 Date: _____ 🕐 Time: _____

📍 Location: _____

Weather Conditions

☀️ ☐   ⛅ ☐   🌤 ☐   🌧 ☐   ☁️ ☐   🌨 ☐   🚩 _____   🌡 _____

Firearm:	
Bullet:	Seating Depth:
Powder:	Grains:
Primer:	
Brass:	
Distance:	

Overall Results

☐ Poor   ☐ Fair   ☐ Good   ☐ Excellent

Notes

_____

_____

_____

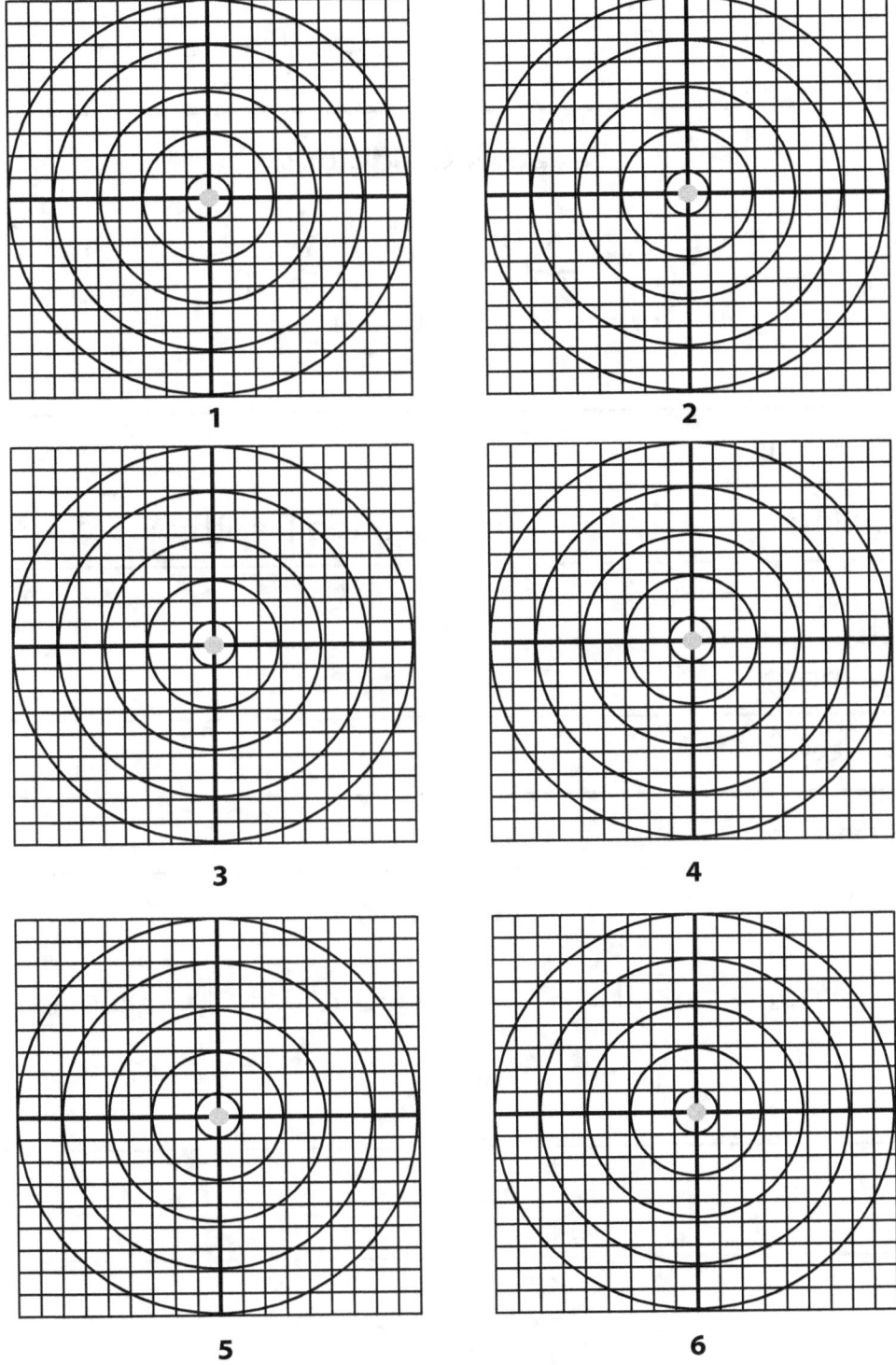

📅 Date: _____ 🕐 Time: _____
📍 Location: _____

Weather Conditions

☀️ ☁️ 🌤️ 🌧️ 🌧️ 🌨️ 🚩 🌡️
☐ ☐ ☐ ☐ ☐ ☐ _____ _____

Firearm:	
Bullet:	Seating Depth:
Powder:	Grains:
Primer:	
Brass:	
Distance:	

Overall Results

☐ Poor   ☐ Fair   ☐ Good   ☐ Excellent

Notes

_____
_____
_____

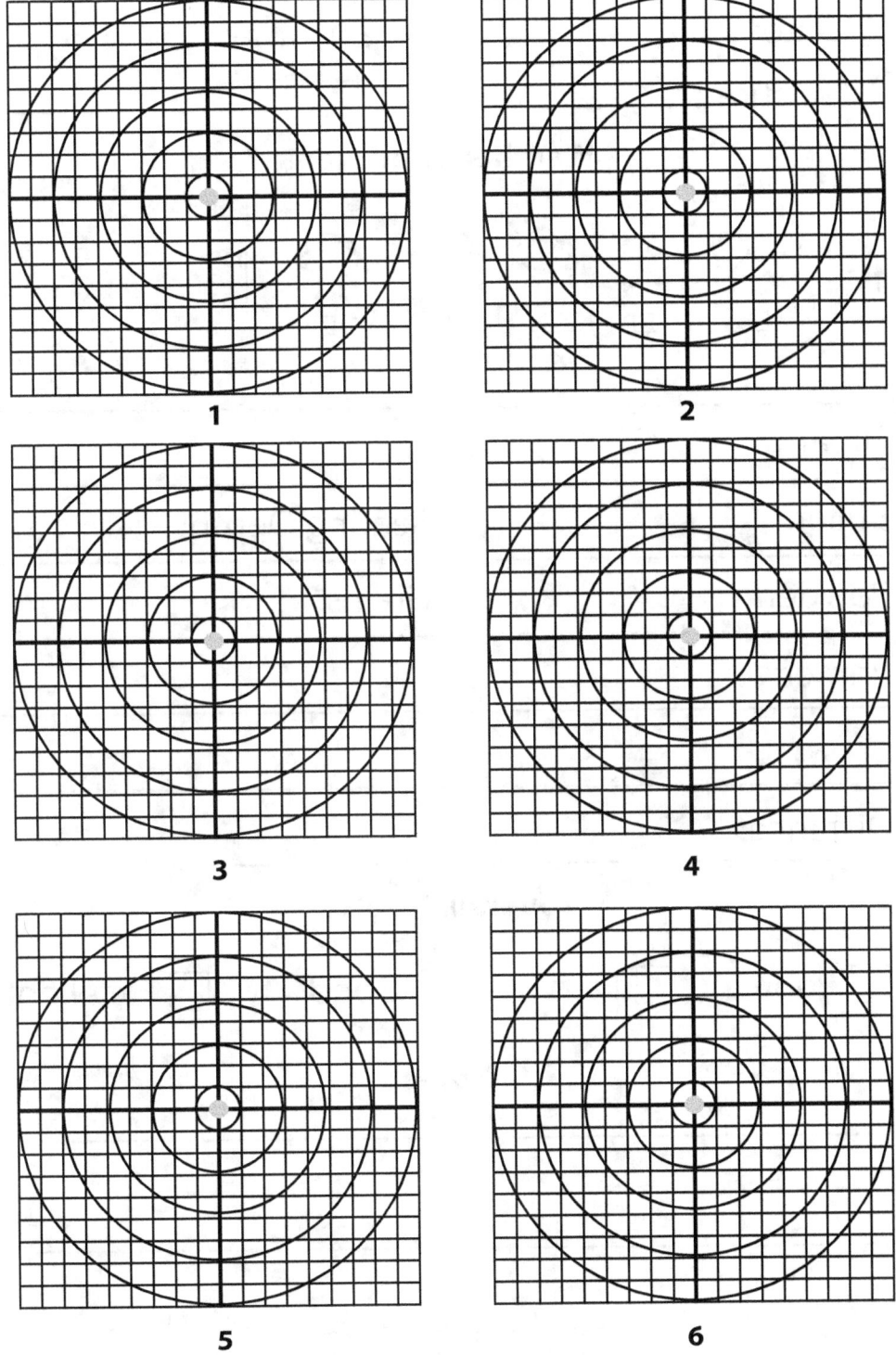

Date: _____ Time: _____

 Location: _____

Weather Conditions

☀ ☁ ⛅ 🌧 🌧 🌨 ⚑ 🌡
☐ ☐ ☐ ☐ ☐ ☐

Firearm:	
Bullet:	Seating Depth:
Powder:	Grains:
Primer:	
Brass:	
Distance:	

Overall Results

☐ Poor   ☐ Fair   ☐ Good   ☐ Excellent

Notes

_____
_____
_____

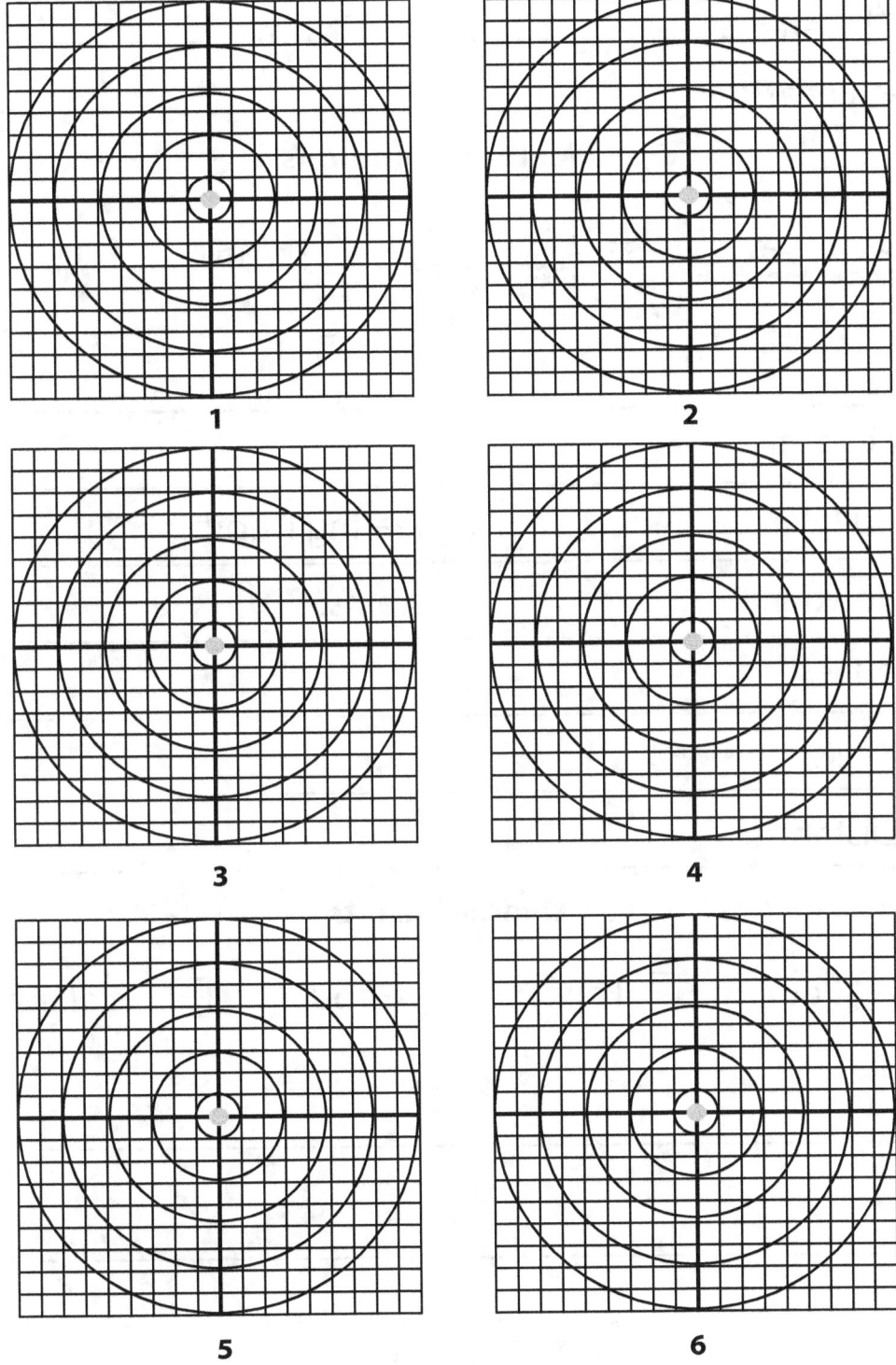

Date: _____   Time: _____

 Location: _____

Weather Conditions

☀ ☁ ⛅ 🌦 🌧 🌨 🚩 🌡
☐ ☐ ☐ ☐ ☐ ☐

Firearm:	
Bullet:	Seating Depth:
Powder:	Grains:
Primer:	
Brass:	
Distance:	

Overall Results

☐ Poor   ☐ Fair   ☐ Good   ☐ Excellent

Notes

_____
_____
_____

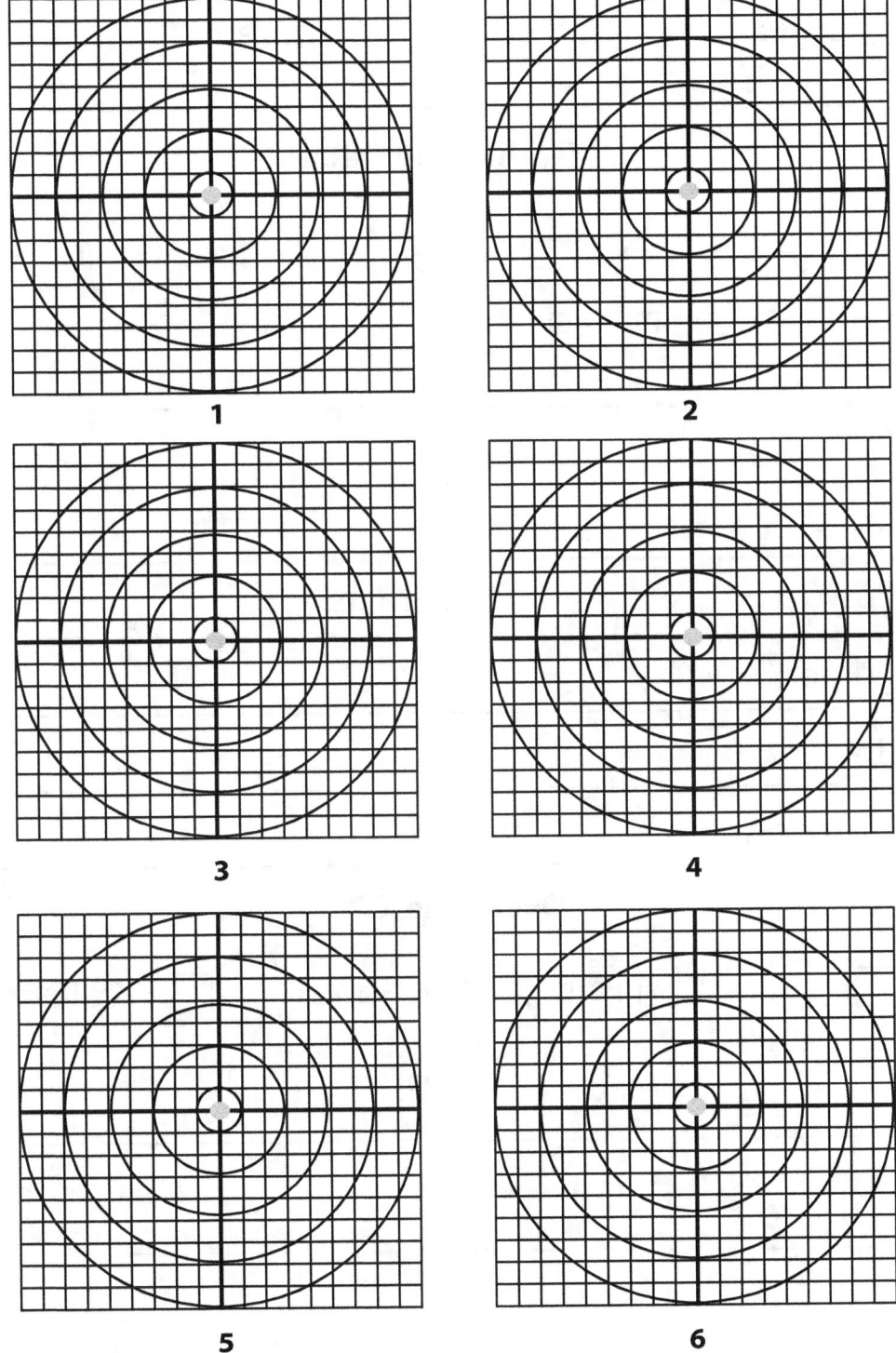

Date: _____ Time: _____

Location: _____

Weather Conditions

☀ ☁ ⛅ 🌧 🌧 🌨 🚩 🌡
☐ ☐ ☐ ☐ ☐ ☐   ___ ___

Firearm:	
Bullet:	Seating Depth:
Powder:	Grains:
Primer:	
Brass:	
Distance:	

Overall Results

☐ Poor   ☐ Fair   ☐ Good   ☐ Excellent

Notes

_____
_____
_____

☆ ☆ ☆ ☆ ☆

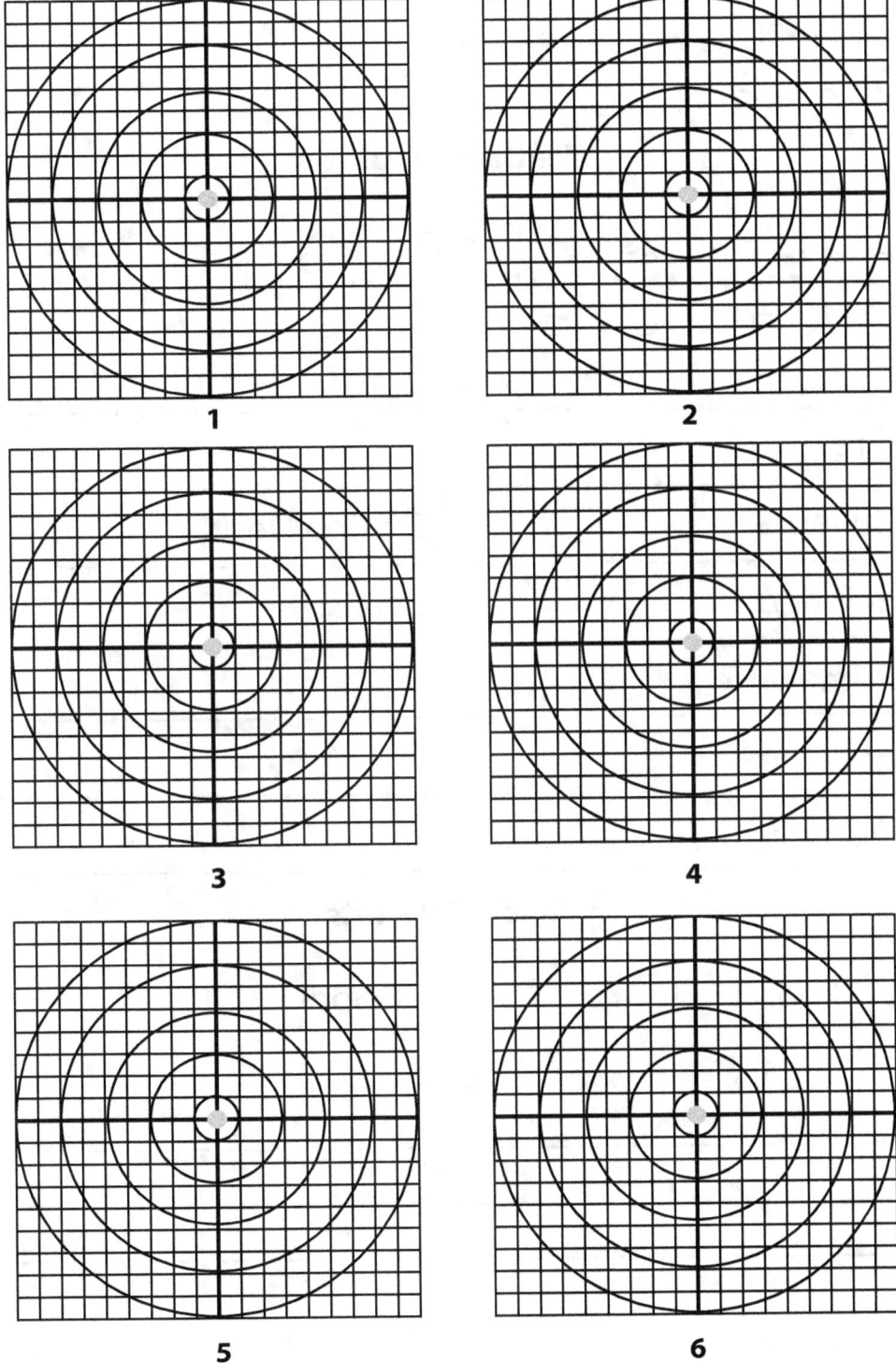

Date: _____ Time: _____

Location: _____

Weather Conditions

☀ ☁ ⛅ 🌧 🌧 🌨 🚩 🌡
☐ ☐ ☐ ☐ ☐ ☐ ___ ___

Firearm:	
Bullet:	Seating Depth:
Powder:	Grains:
Primer:	
Brass:	
Distance:	

Overall Results

☐ Poor   ☐ Fair   ☐ Good   ☐ Excellent

Notes

_____
_____
_____

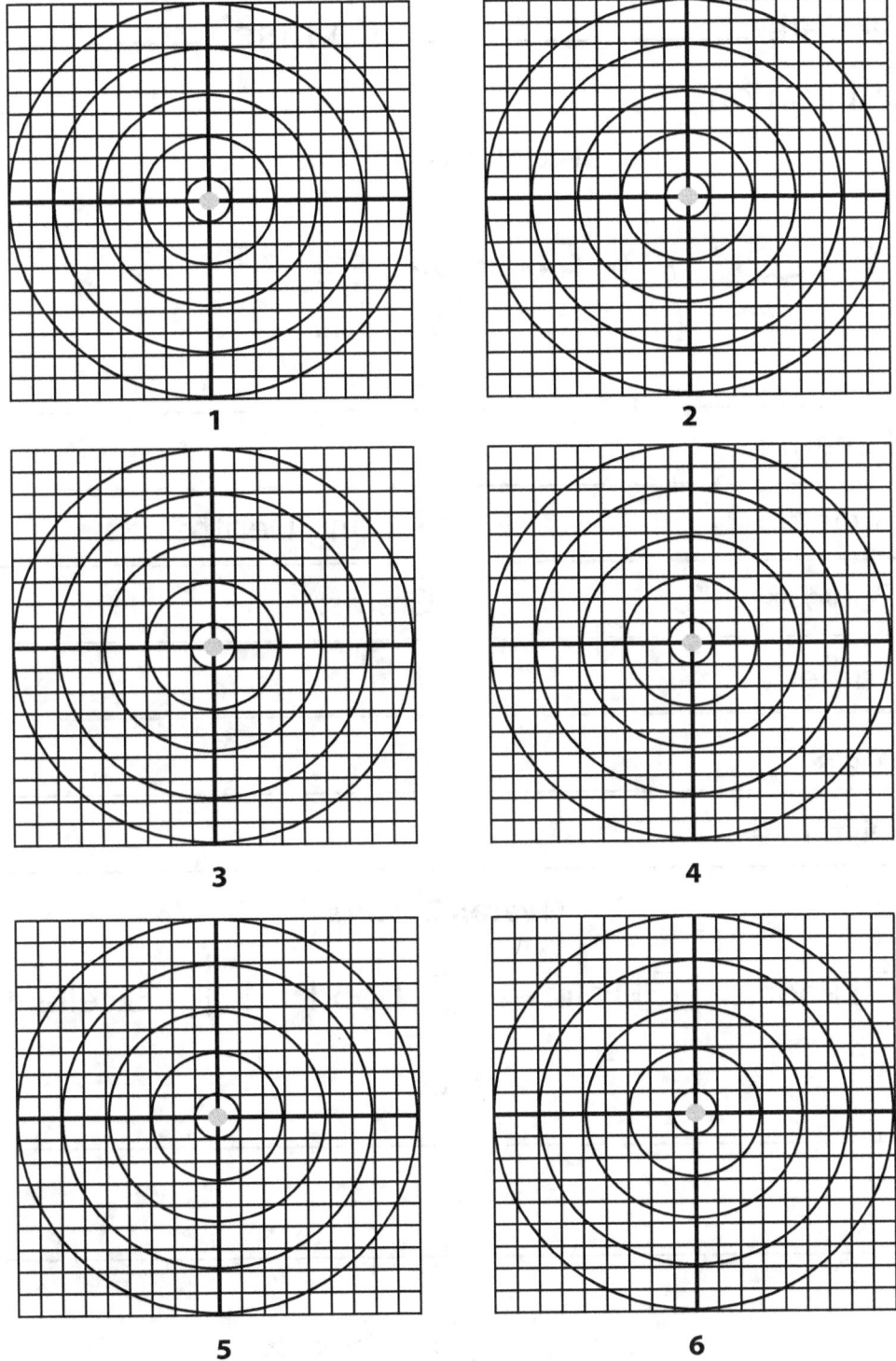

📅 Date: _____ 🕐 Time: _____

📍 Location: _____

Weather Conditions

☀️ ☁️ ⛅ 🌧️ 🌧️ 🌨️ 🚩 🌡️
☐   ☐   ☐   ☐   ☐   ☐   _____   _____

Firearm:	
Bullet:	Seating Depth:
Powder:	Grains:
Primer:	
Brass:	
Distance:	

Overall Results

☐ Poor　　☐ Fair　　☐ Good　　☐ Excellent

Notes

_____

_____

_____

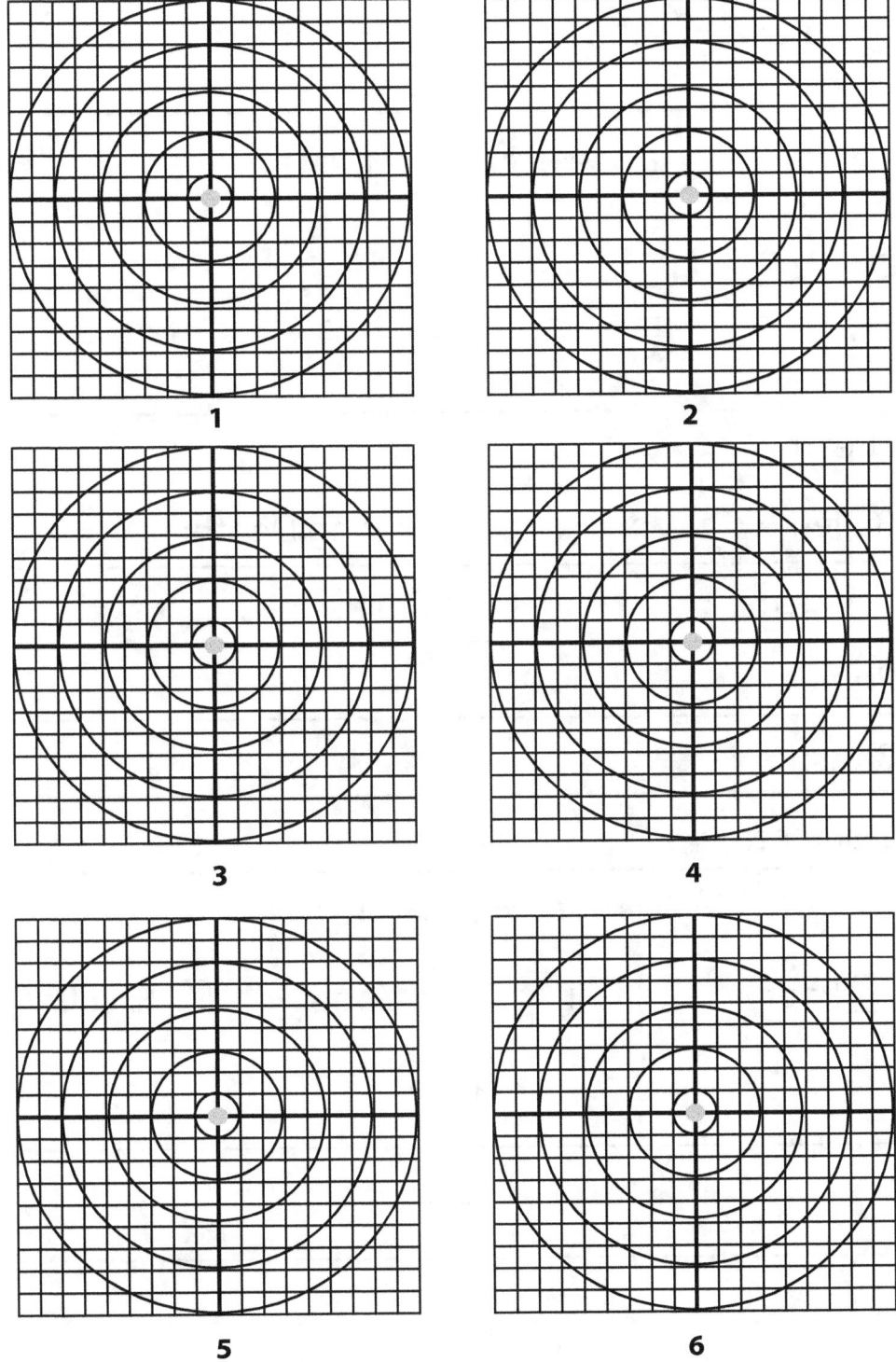

📅 Date: _____ 🕐 Time: _____

📍 Location: _____

Weather Conditions

☀️ ☁️ ⛅ 🌦️ 🌧️ 🌨️ 🚩 🌡️
☐ ☐ ☐ ☐ ☐ ☐ ___ ___

Firearm:	
Bullet:	Seating Depth:
Powder:	Grains:
Primer:	
Brass:	
Distance:	

Overall Results

☐ Poor   ☐ Fair   ☐ Good   ☐ Excellent

Notes

_____

_____

_____

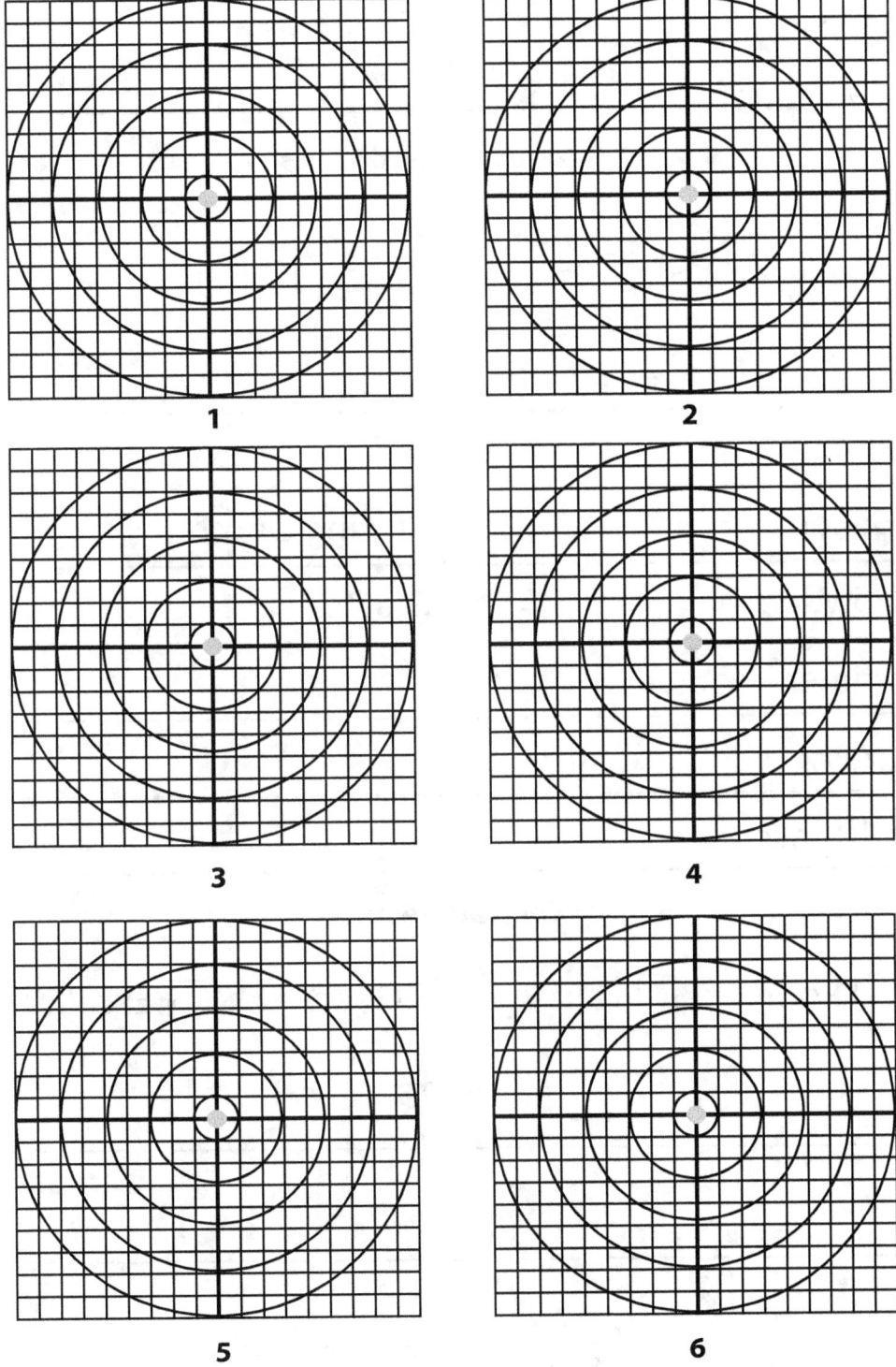

Date: _____ Time: _____

Location: _____

Weather Conditions

☀ ☁ ⛅ 🌧 🌧 🌨 🚩 🌡
☐ ☐ ☐ ☐ ☐ ☐

Firearm:	
Bullet:	Seating Depth:
Powder:	Grains:
Primer:	
Brass:	
Distance:	

Overall Results

☐ Poor   ☐ Fair   ☐ Good   ☐ Excellent

Notes

_____

_____

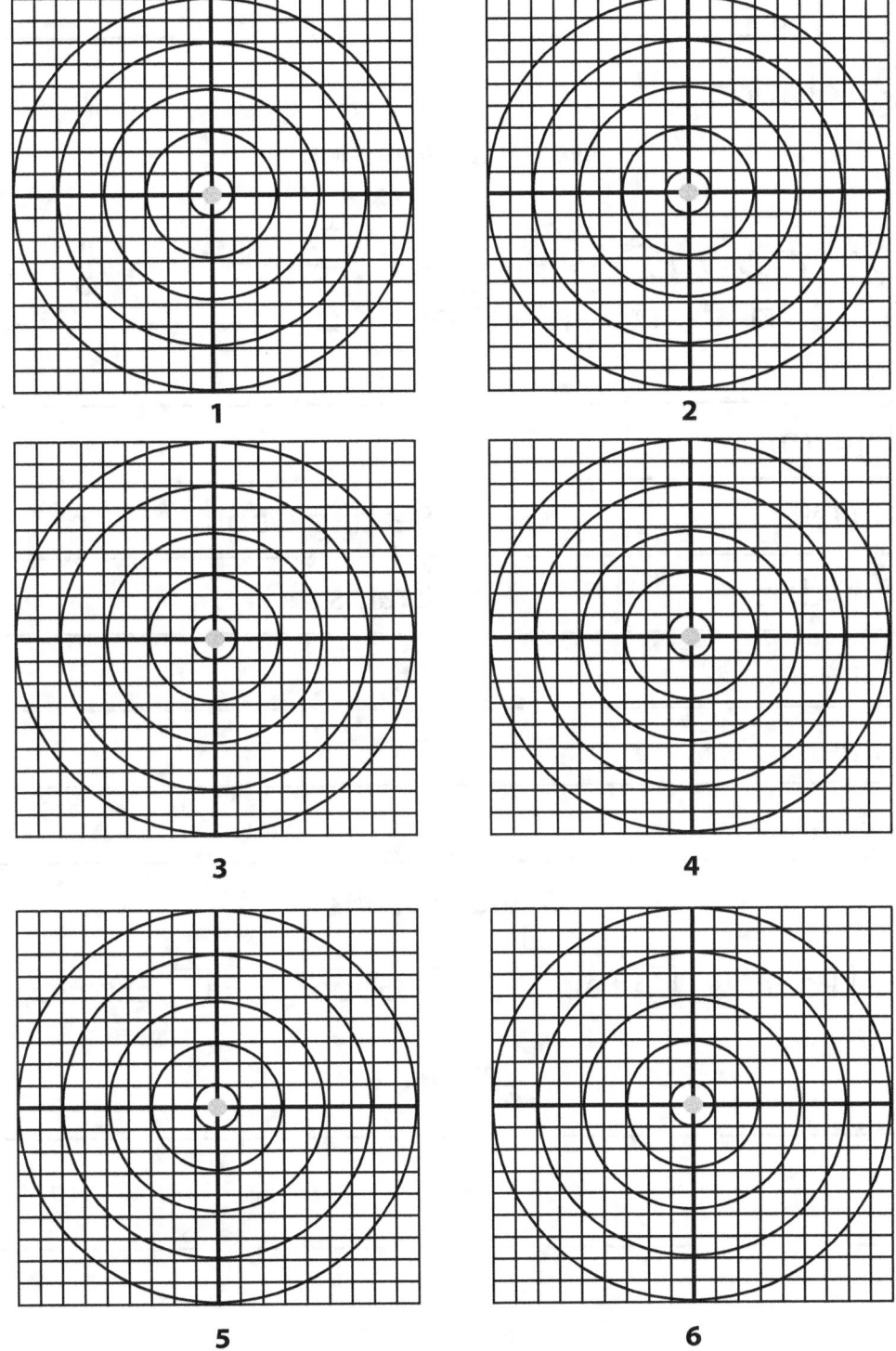

Date: _____ Time: _____
Location: _____

Weather Conditions

☀ ☁ ⛅ 🌦 🌧 🌨 🚩 🌡
☐ ☐ ☐ ☐ ☐ ☐ _____ _____

Firearm:	
Bullet:	Seating Depth:
Powder:	Grains:
Primer:	
Brass:	
Distance:	

Overall Results

☐ Poor   ☐ Fair   ☐ Good   ☐ Excellent

Notes

_____
_____
_____

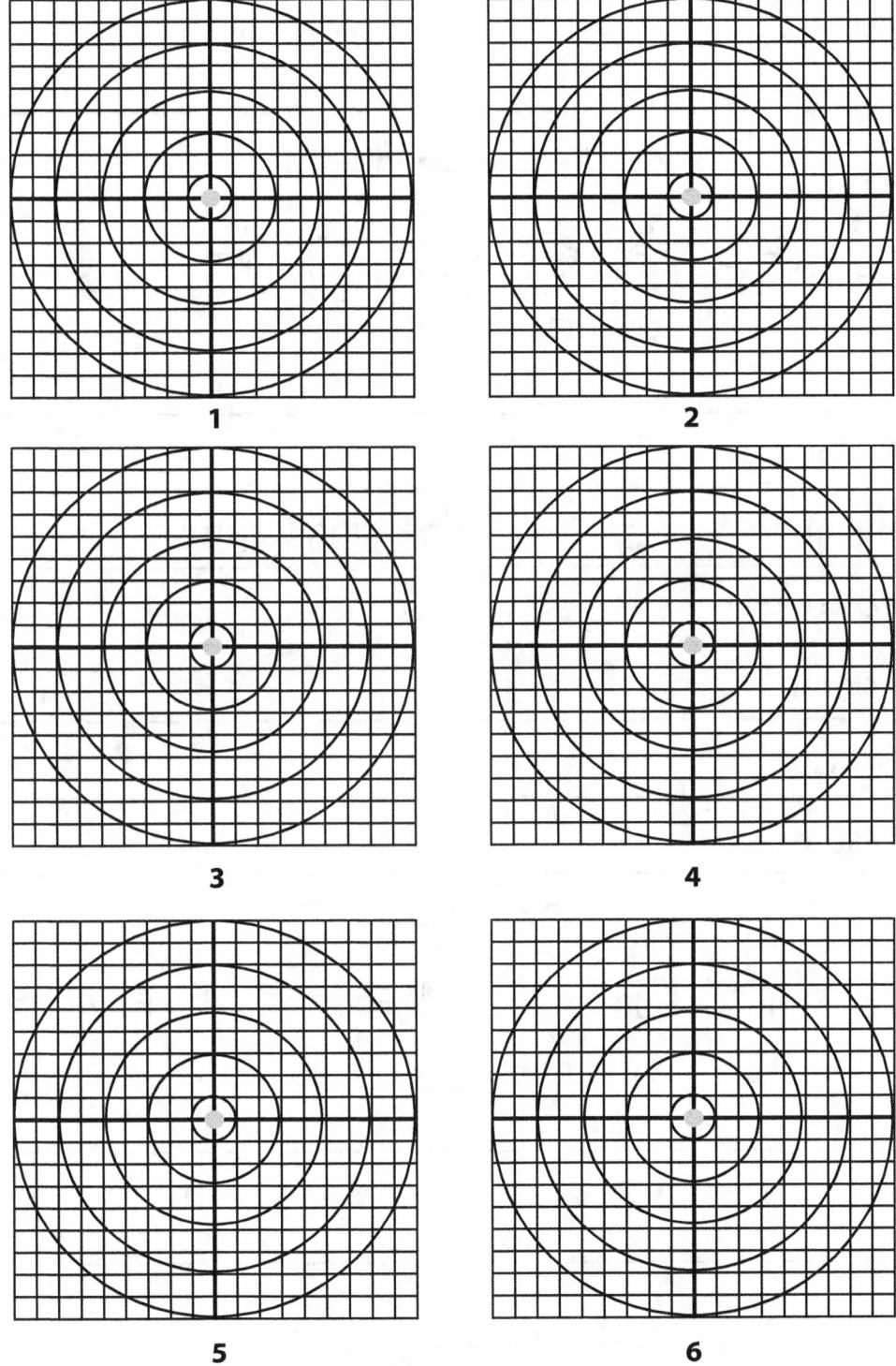

Date: _____   Time: _____

 Location: _____

Weather Conditions

☀ ☐ ☁ ☐ ⛅ ☐ 🌧 ☐ 🌧 ☐ 🌨 ☐ 🚩 ___ 🌡 ___

Firearm:	
Bullet:	Seating Depth:
Powder:	Grains:
Primer:	
Brass:	
Distance:	

Overall Results

☐ Poor ☐ Fair ☐ Good ☐ Excellent

Notes

_____
_____
_____

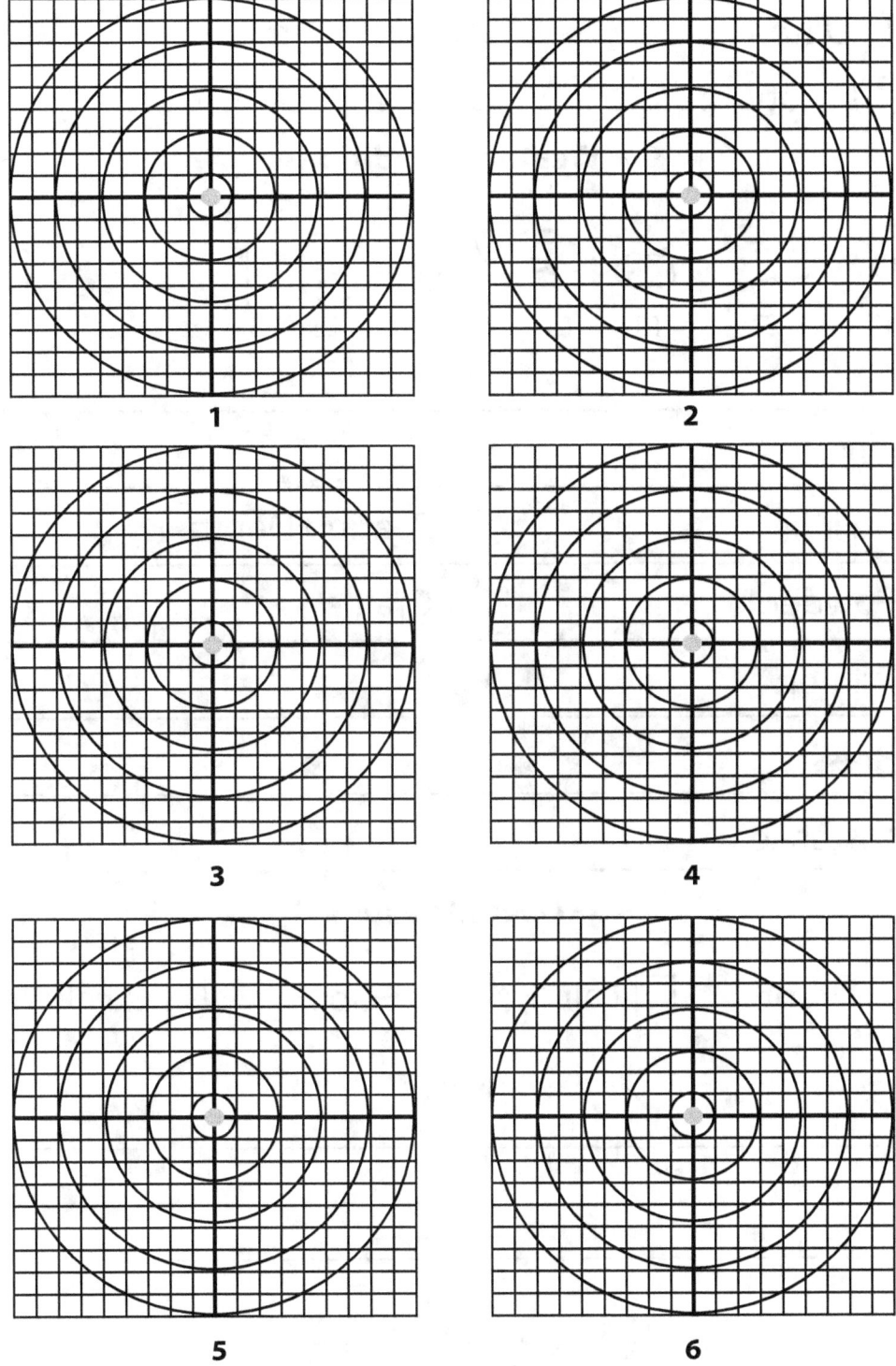

📅 Date: _____ 🕐 Time: _____

📍 Location: _____

Weather Conditions

☀️ ☁️ ⛅ 🌦️ 🌧️ 🌨️ 🚩 🌡️
☐ ☐ ☐ ☐ ☐ ☐   _____

Firearm:	
Bullet:	Seating Depth:
Powder:	Grains:
Primer:	
Brass:	
Distance:	

Overall Results

☐ Poor   ☐ Fair   ☐ Good   ☐ Excellent

Notes

_____

_____

_____

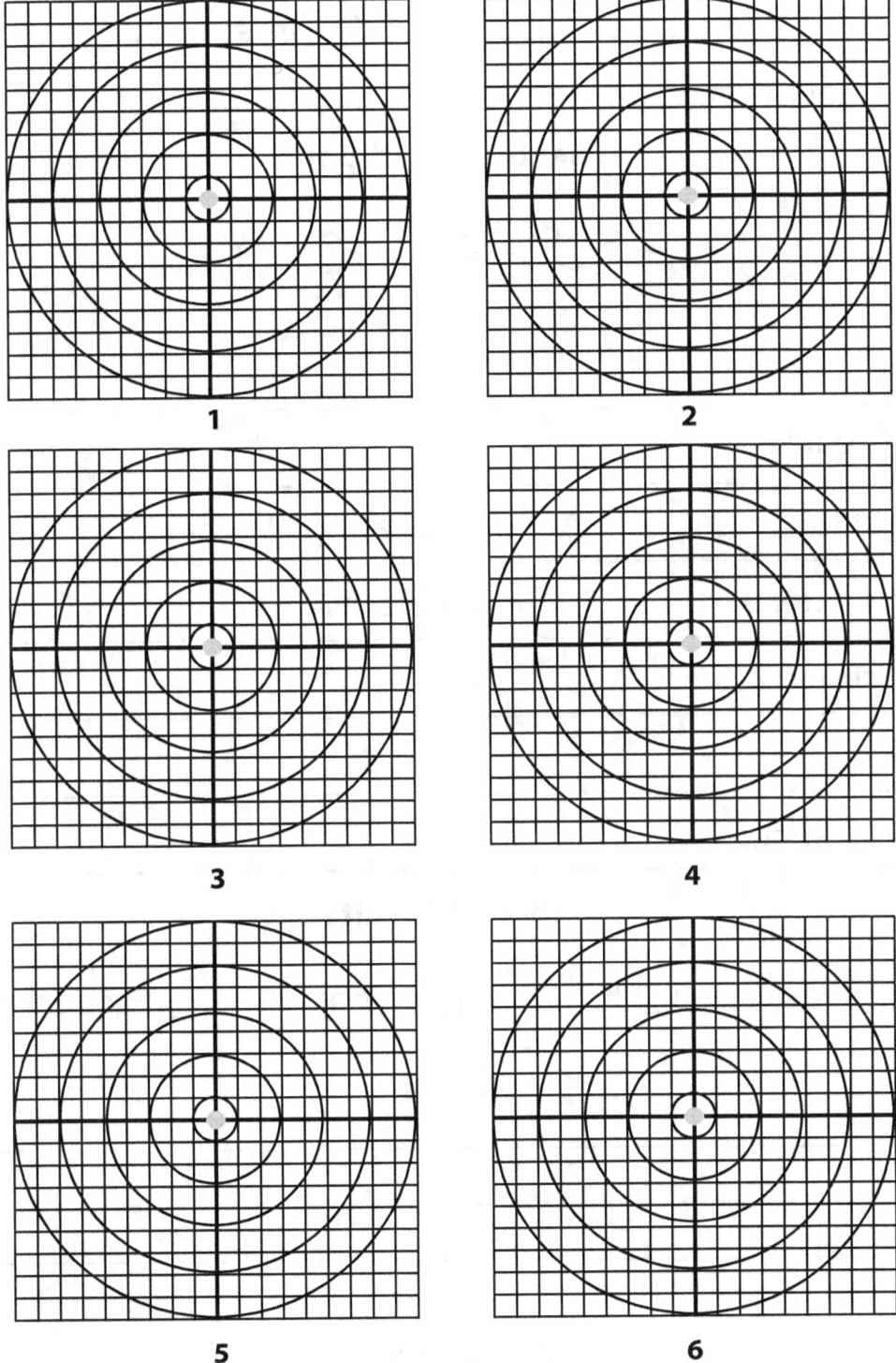

Date: _____ Time: _____

Location: _____

Weather Conditions

☀ ☁ ⛅ 🌧 🌦 🌨 🚩 🌡
☐ ☐ ☐ ☐ ☐ ☐

Firearm:	
Bullet:	Seating Depth:
Powder:	Grains:
Primer:	
Brass:	
Distance:	

Overall Results

☐ Poor ☐ Fair ☐ Good ☐ Excellent

Notes

_____

_____

_____

☆ ☆ ☆ ☆ ☆

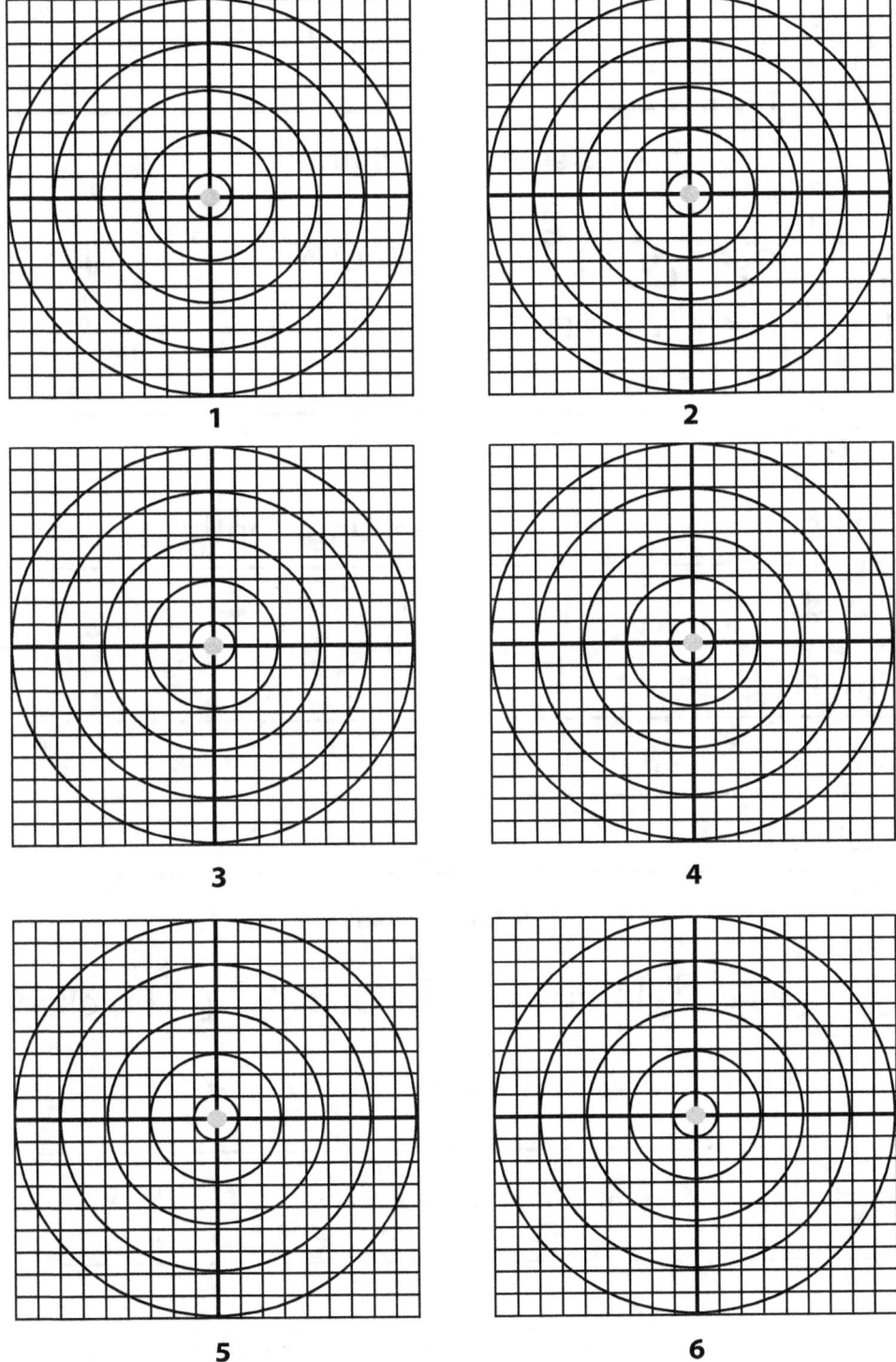

📅 Date: _____   🕐 Time: _____

📍 Location: _____

Weather Conditions

☀️ ☐   ⛅ ☐   🌤 ☐   🌦 ☐   🌧 ☐   🌨 ☐   🚩   🌡

Firearm:	
Bullet:	Seating Depth:
Powder:	Grains:
Primer:	
Brass:	
Distance:	

Overall Results

☐ Poor   ☐ Fair   ☐ Good   ☐ Excellent

Notes

_____

_____

_____

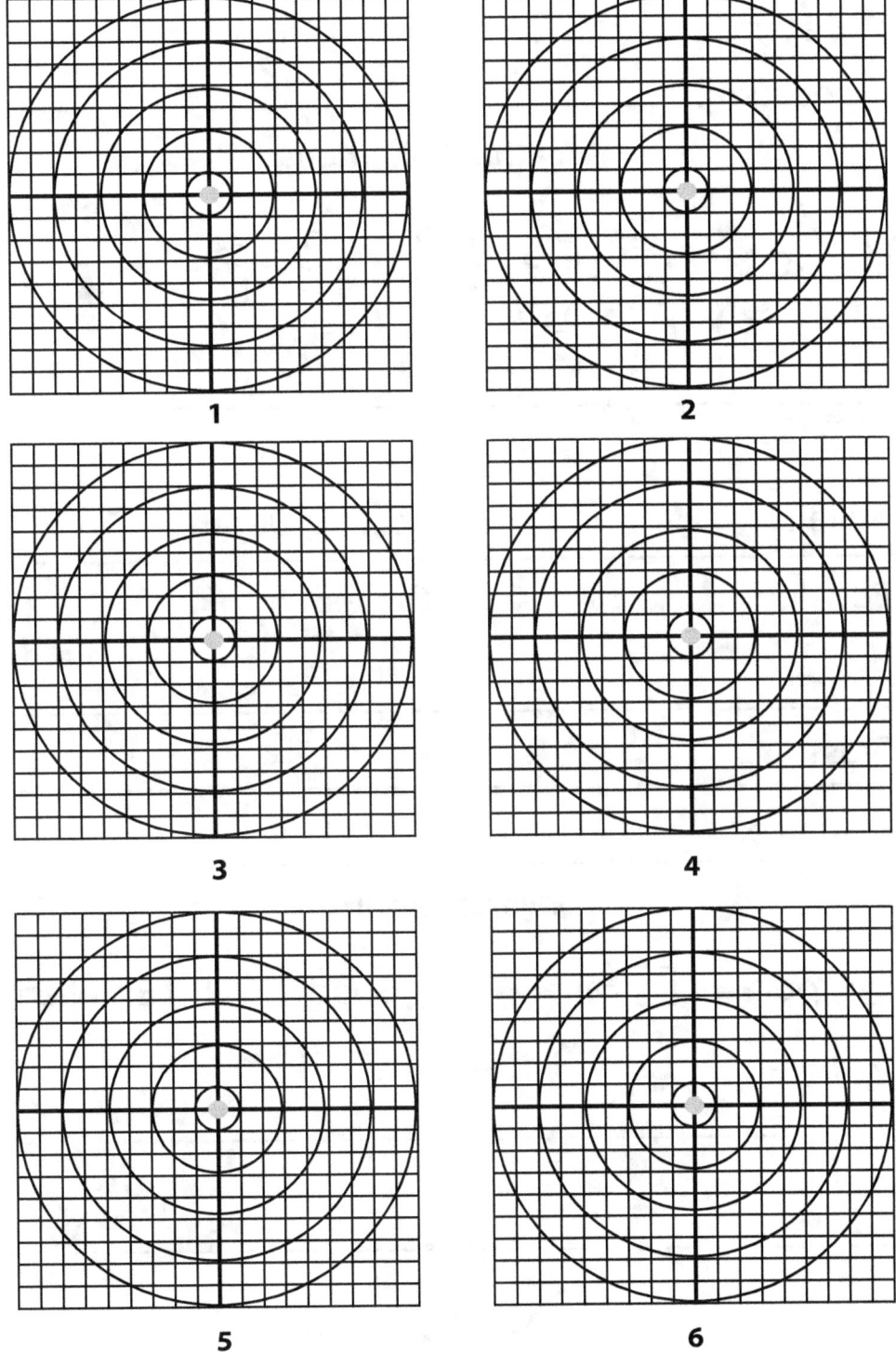

📅 Date: _____ 🕐 Time: _____

📍 Location: _____

Weather Conditions

☀️ ☁️ ⛅ 🌧️ 🌦️ 🌨️ 🚩 🌡️
☐   ☐   ☐   ☐   ☐   ☐

Firearm:	
Bullet:	Seating Depth:
Powder:	Grains:
Primer:	
Brass:	
Distance:	

Overall Results

☐ Poor   ☐ Fair   ☐ Good   ☐ Excellent

Notes

_____

_____

_____

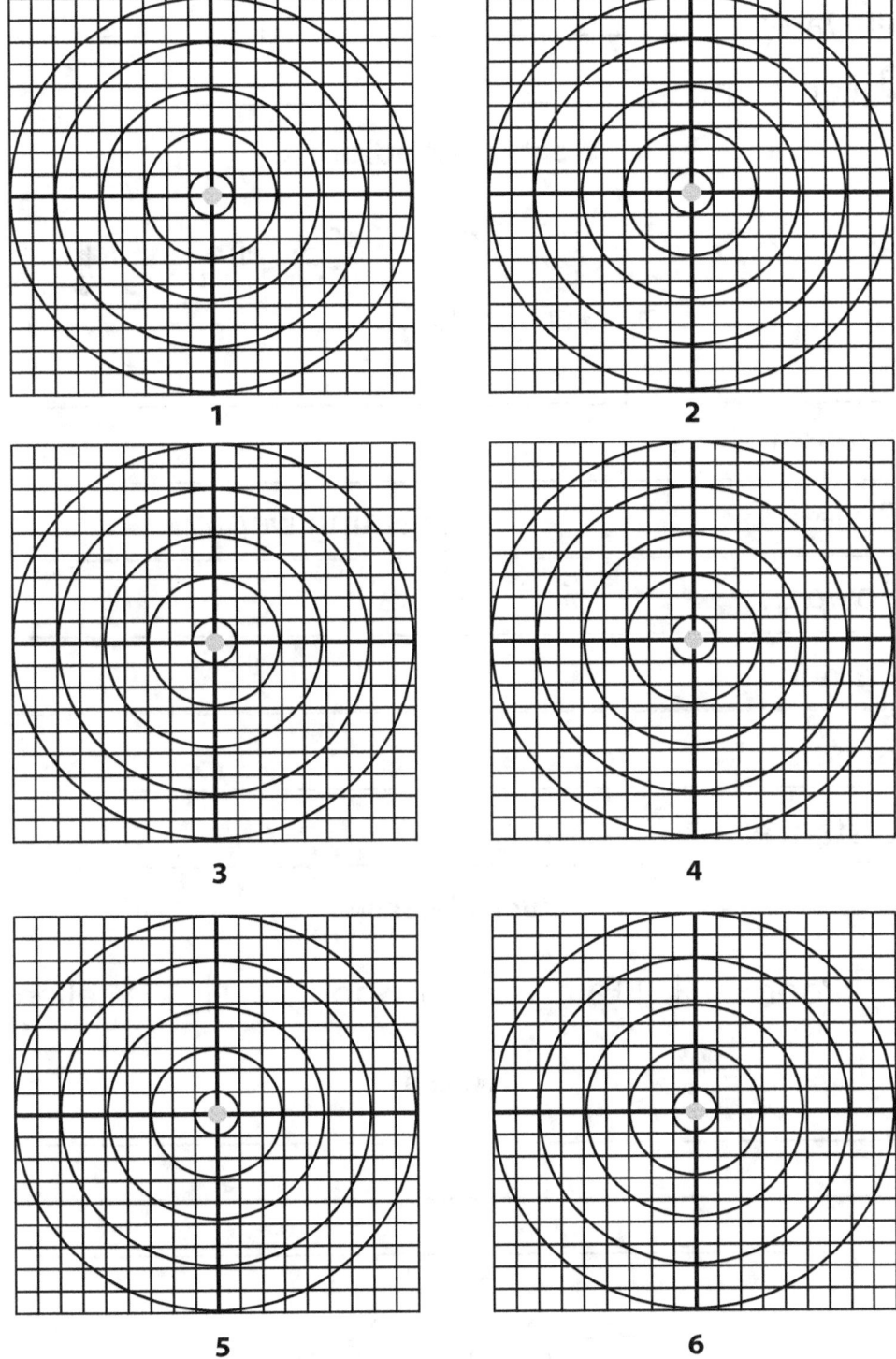

Date: _____ Time: _____

Location: _____

Weather Conditions

☀ ☁ 🌤 🌧 🌦 🌨 🚩 🌡
☐ ☐ ☐ ☐ ☐ ☐ ☐ _____

Firearm:	
Bullet:	Seating Depth:
Powder:	Grains:
Primer:	
Brass:	
Distance:	

Overall Results

☐ Poor   ☐ Fair   ☐ Good   ☐ Excellent

Notes

_____

_____

_____

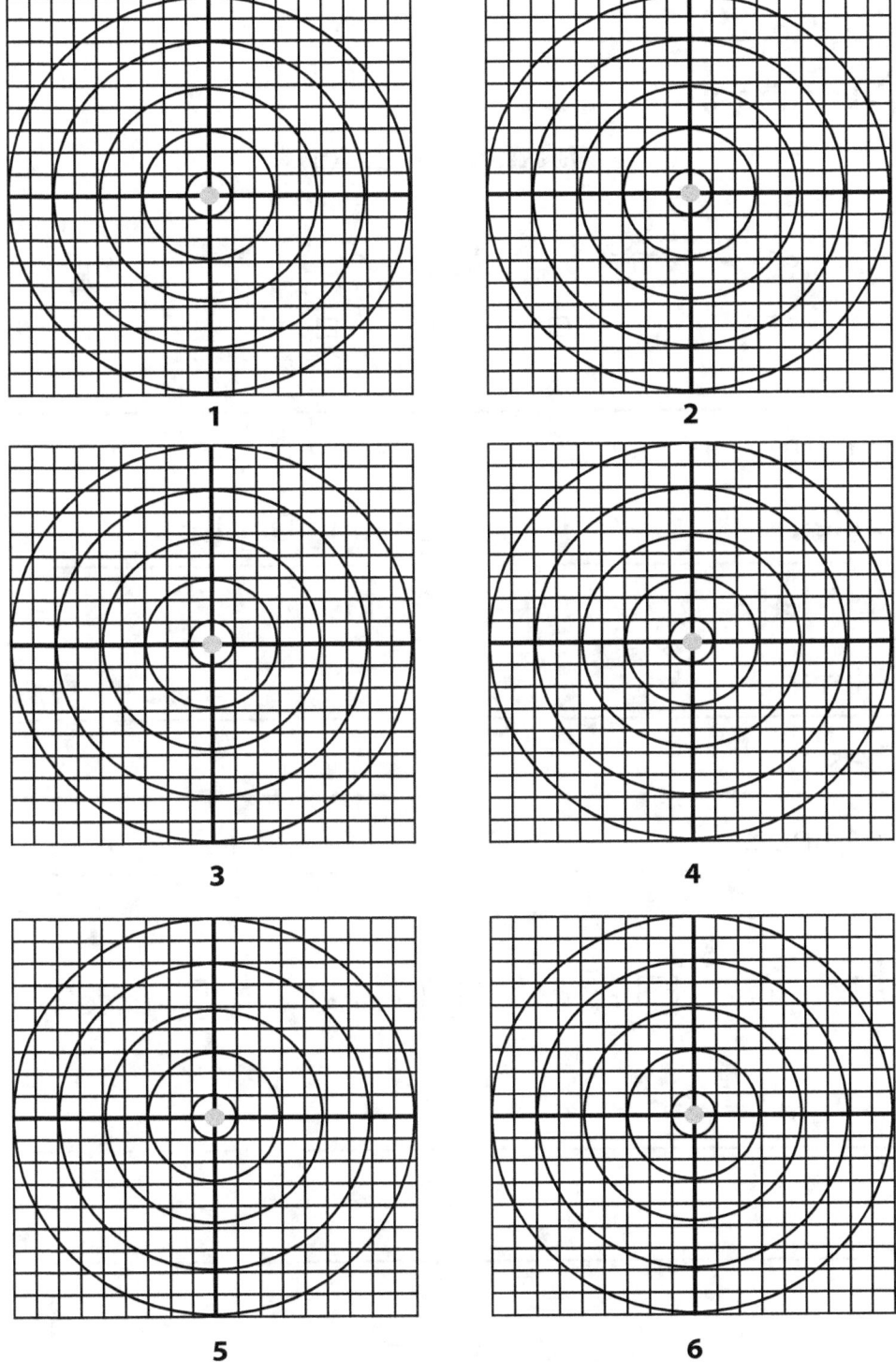

Date: _____   Time: _____

Location: _____

Weather Conditions

☀ ☁ 🌥 🌦 🌧 🌨 🚩 🌡
☐   ☐   ☐   ☐   ☐   ☐   ___   ___

Firearm:	
Bullet:	Seating Depth:
Powder:	Grains:
Primer:	
Brass:	
Distance:	

Overall Results

☐ Poor   ☐ Fair   ☐ Good   ☐ Excellent

Notes

_____
_____
_____

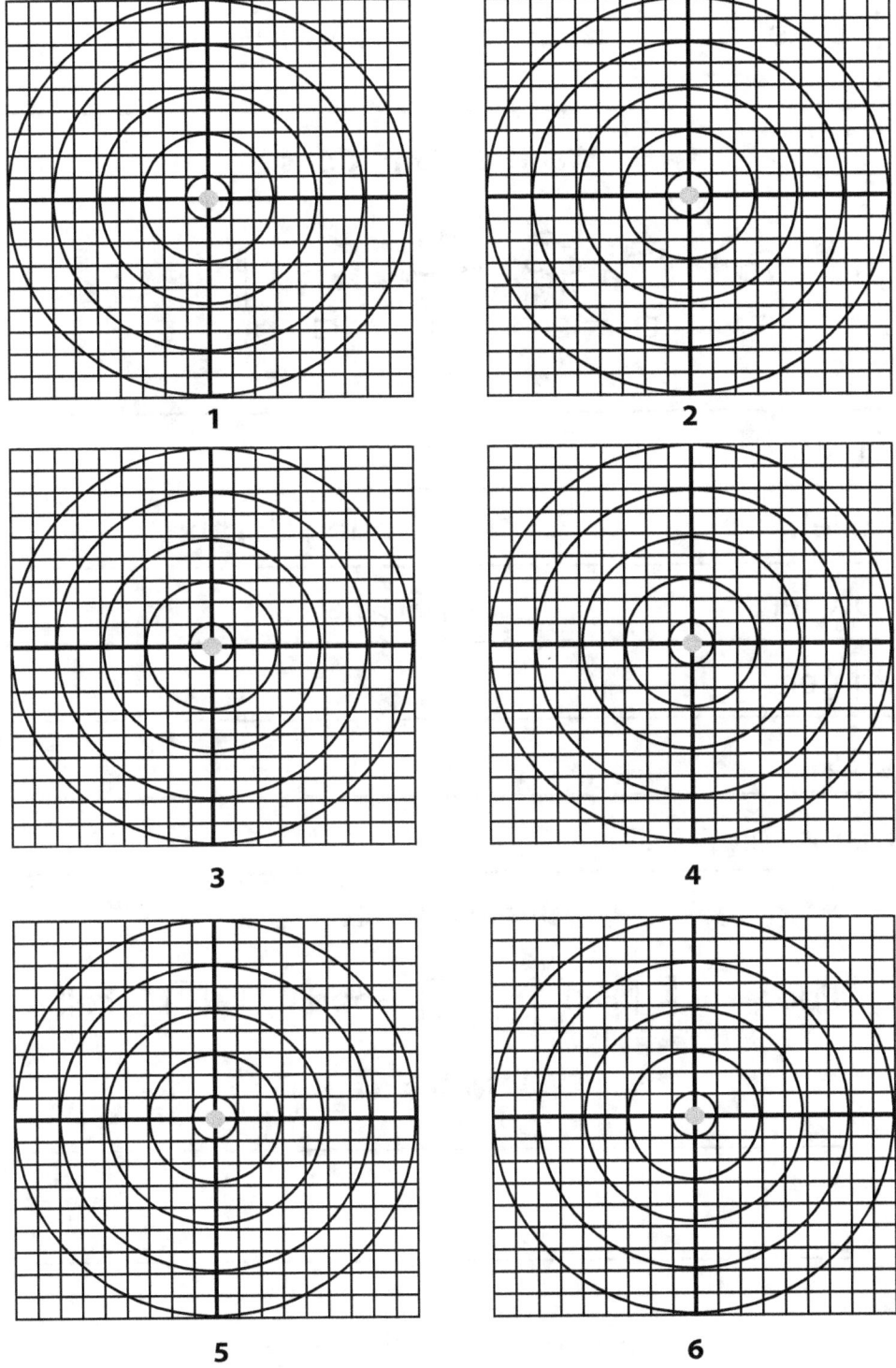

Date: _____ Time: _____
Location: _____

Weather Conditions

☀ ☁ ⛅ 🌧 🌧 🌨 🚩 🌡
☐ ☐ ☐ ☐ ☐ ☐ _____ _____

Firearm:	
Bullet:	Seating Depth:
Powder:	Grains:
Primer:	
Brass:	
Distance:	

Overall Results

☐ Poor   ☐ Fair   ☐ Good   ☐ Excellent

Notes

_____
_____
_____

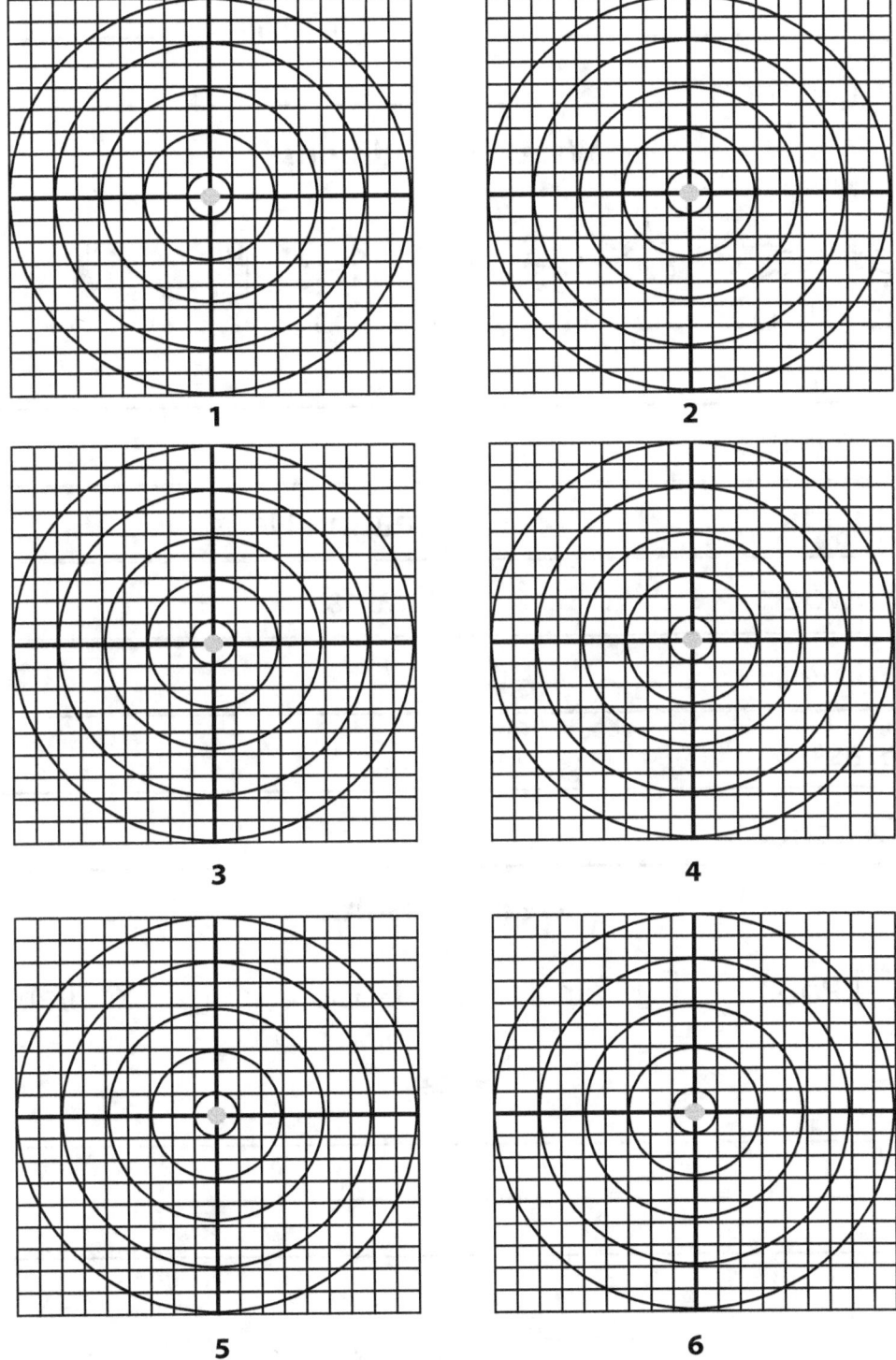

Date: _____ Time: _____
 Location: _____

Weather Conditions

☀ ☁ ⛅ 🌧 🌧 🌨 🚩 🌡
☐ ☐ ☐ ☐ ☐ ☐ ____ ____

Firearm:	
Bullet:	Seating Depth:
Powder:	Grains:
Primer:	
Brass:	
Distance:	

Overall Results

☐ Poor   ☐ Fair   ☐ Good   ☐ Excellent

Notes

_____
_____
_____

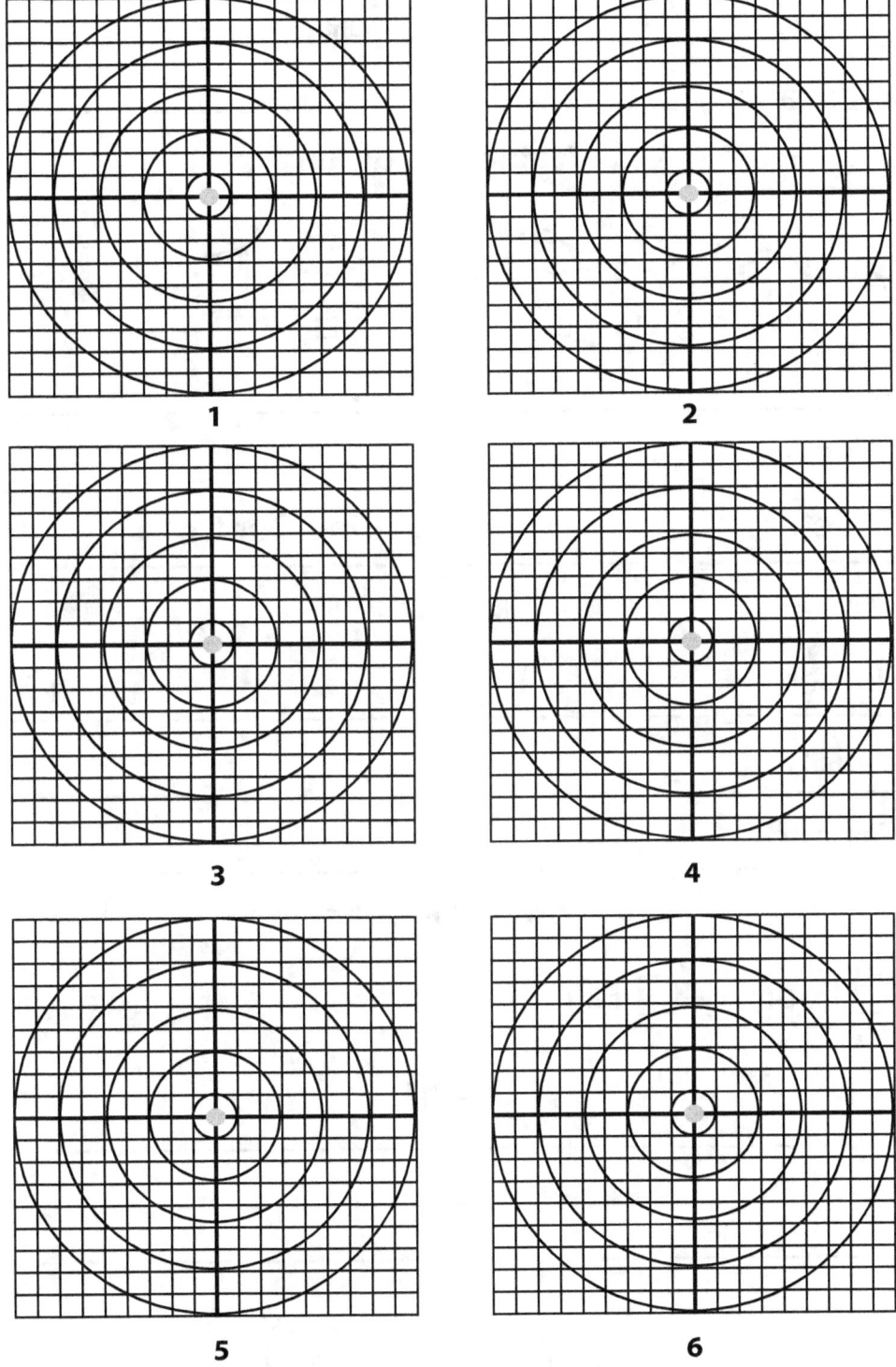

📅 Date: _____ 🕐 Time: _____

📍 Location: _____

Weather Conditions

☀️ ☁️ ⛅ 🌧️ 🌦️ 🌨️ 🚩 🌡️
☐ ☐ ☐ ☐ ☐ ☐

Firearm:	
Bullet:	Seating Depth:
Powder:	Grains:
Primer:	
Brass:	
Distance:	

Overall Results

☐ Poor   ☐ Fair   ☐ Good   ☐ Excellent

Notes

_____

_____

_____

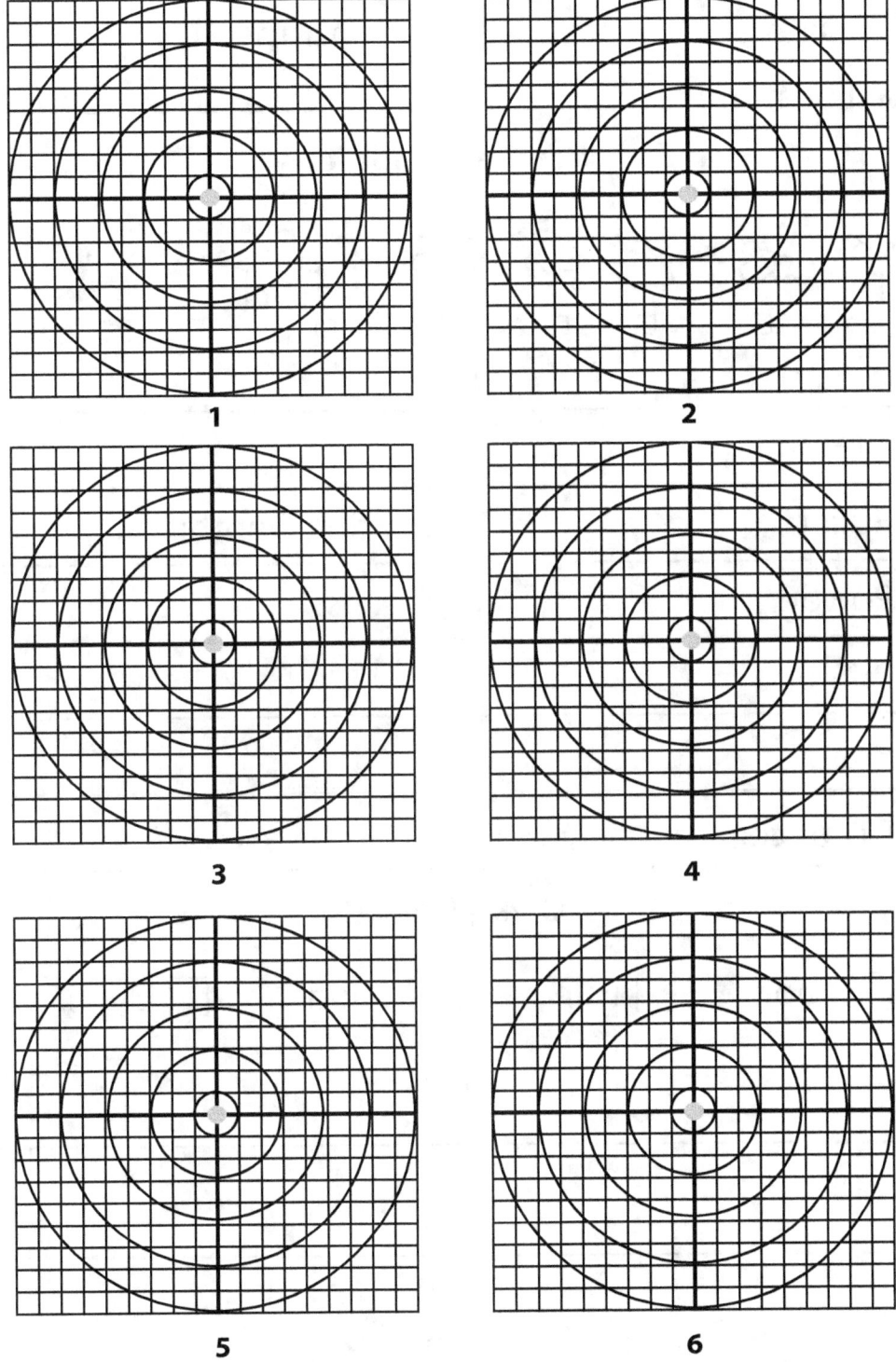

📅 Date: _____ 🕐 Time: _____

📍 Location: _____

Weather Conditions

☀ ☁ ⛅ 🌧 🌧 🌨 🚩 🌡
☐   ☐   ☐   ☐   ☐   ☐

Firearm:	
Bullet:	Seating Depth:
Powder:	Grains:
Primer:	
Brass:	
Distance:	

Overall Results

☐ Poor   ☐ Fair   ☐ Good   ☐ Excellent

Notes

_____
_____
_____

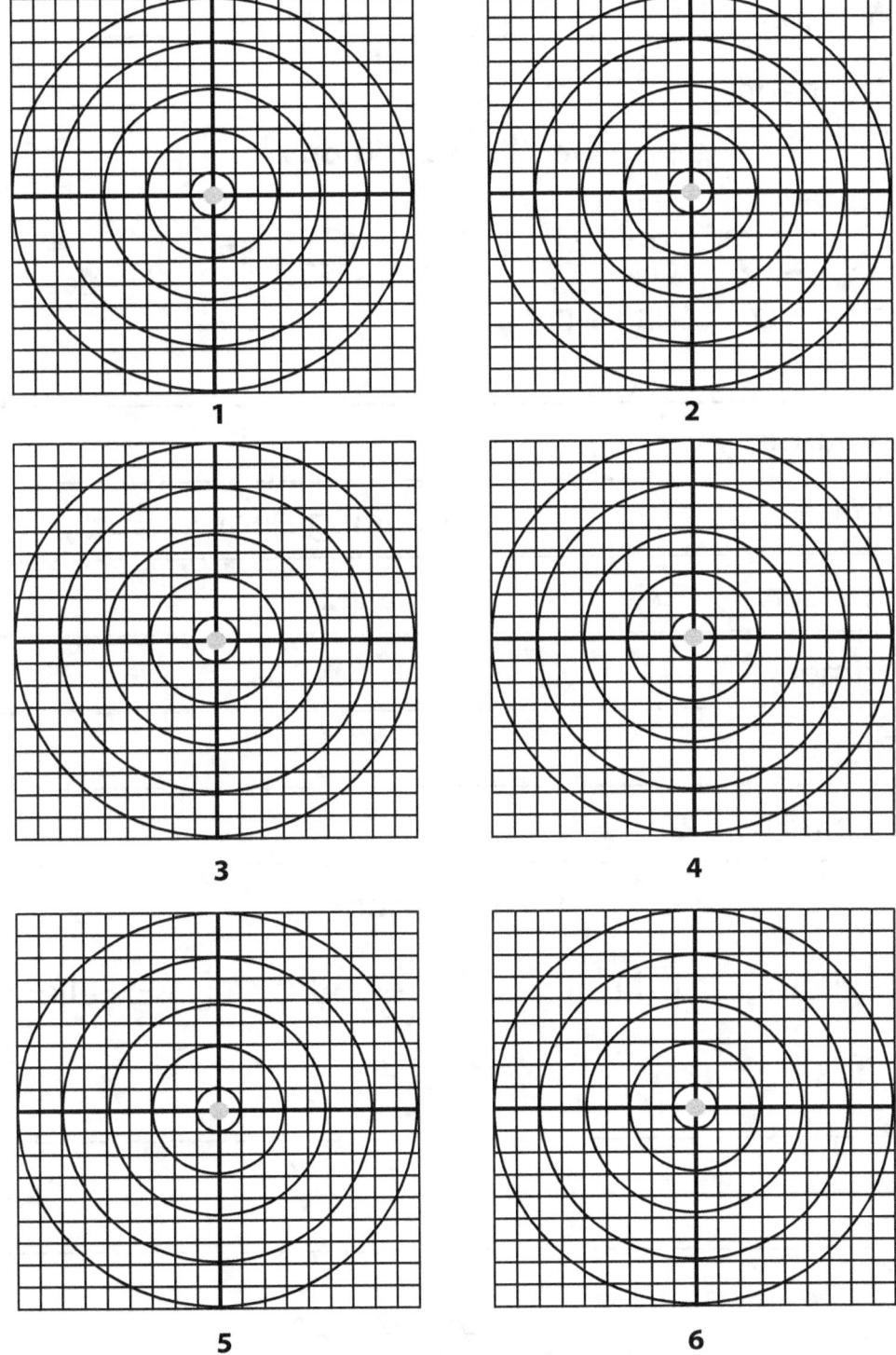

Date: _____ Time: _____

 Location: _____

Weather Conditions

☀ ☁ ⛅ 🌧 🌧 🌨 🚩 🌡
☐ ☐ ☐ ☐ ☐ ☐

Firearm:	
Bullet:	Seating Depth:
Powder:	Grains:
Primer:	
Brass:	
Distance:	

Overall Results

☐ Poor   ☐ Fair   ☐ Good   ☐ Excellent

Notes

_____
_____
_____

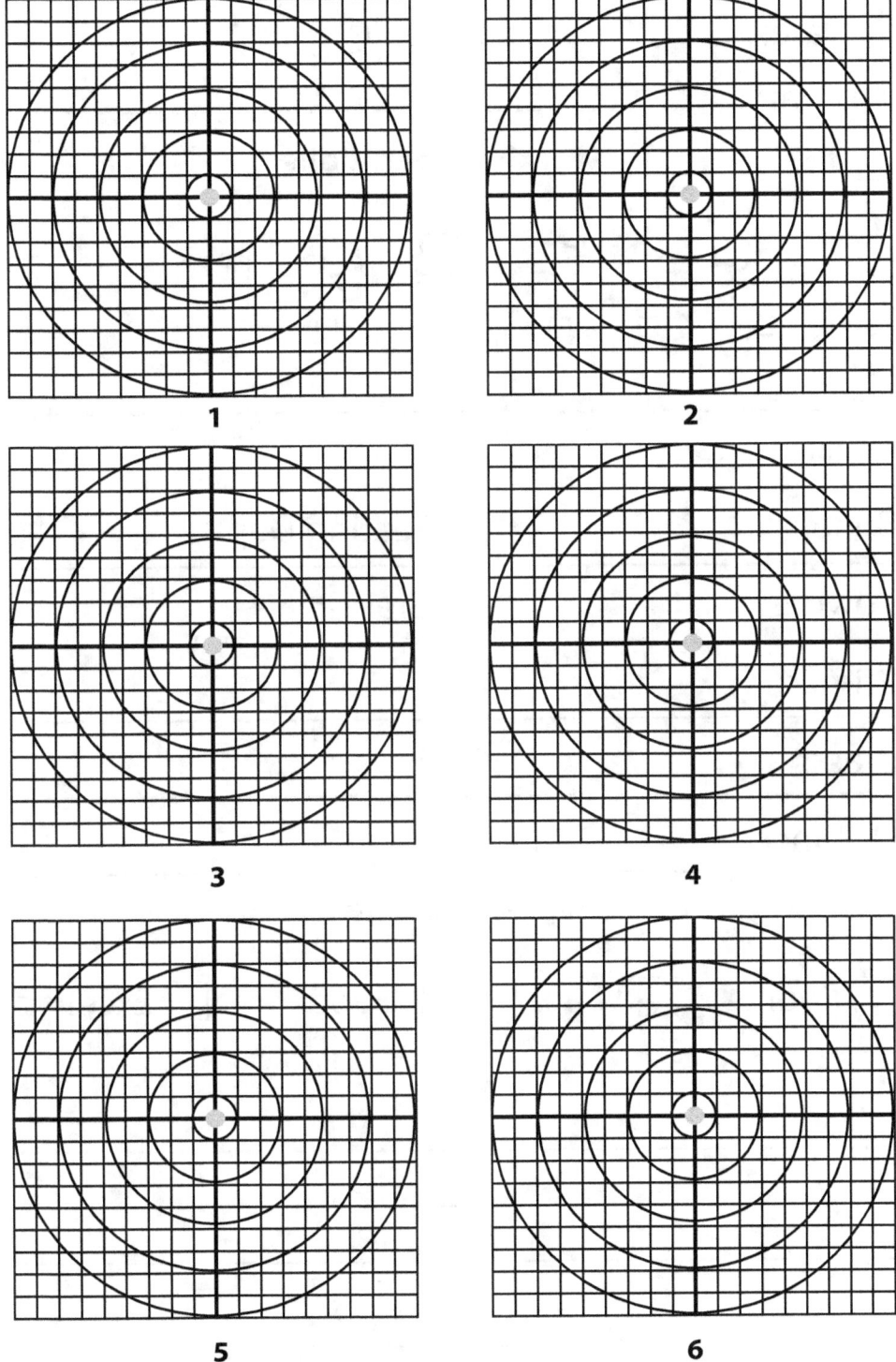

📅 Date: _____   🕐 Time: _____

📍 Location: _____

Weather Conditions

☀ ☁ 🌤 🌧 🌧 🌨 🚩 🌡
☐   ☐   ☐   ☐   ☐   ☐

Firearm:	
Bullet:	Seating Depth:
Powder:	Grains:
Primer:	
Brass:	
Distance:	

Overall Results

☐ Poor   ☐ Fair   ☐ Good   ☐ Excellent

Notes

_____

_____

_____

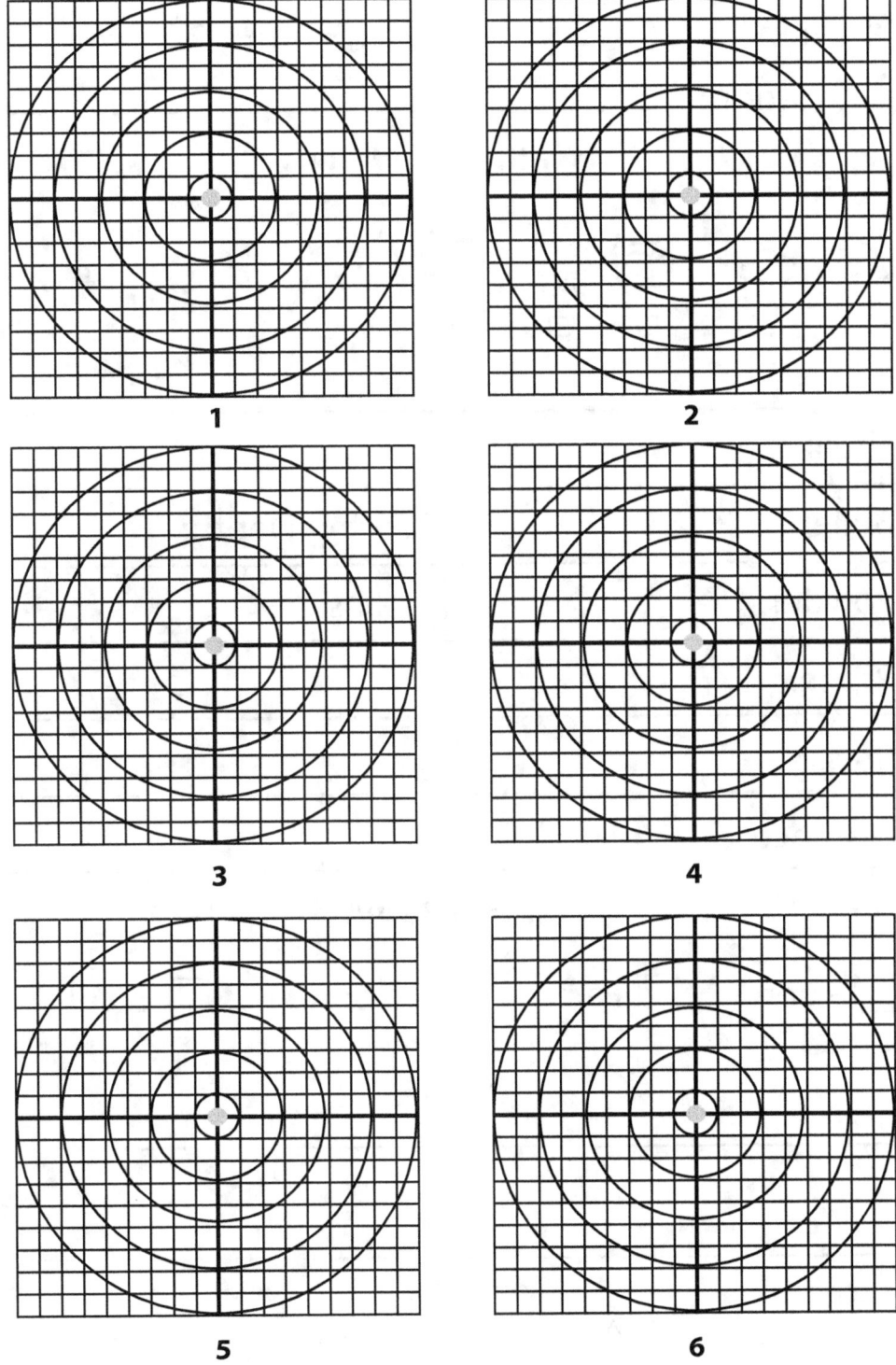

📅 Date: _____ 🕐 Time: _____

📍 Location: _____

Weather Conditions

☀️ ☁️ ⛅ 🌧️ 🌧️ 🌨️ 🚩 🌡️
☐   ☐   ☐   ☐   ☐   ☐   _____

Firearm:	
Bullet:	Seating Depth:
Powder:	Grains:
Primer:	
Brass:	
Distance:	

Overall Results

☐ Poor   ☐ Fair   ☐ Good   ☐ Excellent

Notes

_____
_____
_____

www.ingramcontent.com/pod-product-compliance
Lightning Source LLC
Chambersburg PA
CBHW071125130526
44590CB00056B/2399